Concord Makes Strength
Essays in Reformed Ecumenism

edited by
John W. Coakley

Copyright 2002 by Wm.B.Eerdmans Publishing Co.
255 Jefferson Ave., S.E., Grand Rapids, Mich., 49503

Printed in the United States of America

ISBN 0-8028-0979-0

The Historical Series of the Reformed Church in America

No. 41

Concord Makes Strength
Essays in Reformed Ecumenism

edited by
John W. Coakley

Wm. B. Eerdmans Publishing Co.
Grand Rapids, Michigan

The Historical Series of the Reformed Church in America

The series was inaugurated in 1968 by the General Synod of the Reformed Church in America acting through the Commission on History to communicate the church's heritage and collective memory and to reflect on our identity and mission, encouraging historical scholarship which informs both church and academy.

General Editor

The Reverend Donald J. Bruggink, Ph.D.
Western Theological Seminary

Commission on History

James Brumm, M.Div., Blooming Grove, New York
Lynn Japinga, Ph.D., Hope College, Holland, Michigan
Melody Meeter, M.Div., Brooklyn, New York
Jesus Serrano, B.A., Norwalk, California
Robert Terwilliger, M.Div., Kalamazoo, Michigan
Jeffrey Tyler, Ph.D., Hope College, Holland, Michigan

Contents

Preface

The stated purpose of the Center for Reformed Church Studies at New Brunswick Theological Seminary is "to promote reflection on the history, life and witness of the Reformed Church in America and of the broader Reformed tradition." The essays in this volume, which originated as lectures at a conference held to inaugurate the center, on 30 April and 1 May, 2001, constitute a wonderful array of examples of such reflection. I take pleasure in presenting them now in published form, with the hope that they will be of help to those Christians, Reformed and otherwise, who struggle with ecumenical encounter even as they confess, when they say the Nicene Creed, that the oneness of the church is of the essence of the faith.

Thanks are in order to several persons for helping bring this project to completion: first of all to Susan Hasner the program coordinator for the center, who has, more than anyone else, kept the project on track; to Paul Fries and Douglas Fromm for their ideas and substantial efforts in the initial planning of the conference; to Renée House, Hak Joon Lee, David Waanders, Paul Janssen, Jennifer Reece, Margaret Coakley, and particularly Everett Zabriskie and Sandra Sheppard for their work in making the conference a success; to Norman Kansfield for his consistent support and advice; to Marsha Blake and SoAe Lee for library research assistance; to Donald Bruggink, Laurie Baron, the members of the RCA Historical Commission and above all Russell Gasero, who made it possible to bring this book to press with what in the circumstances has been nothing less than lightning speed.

John Coakley
Easter, 2002

Contributors

Karel Blei is retired general secretary of the Dutch Reformed Church.

Anna Case-Winters is associate professor of theology at McCormick Theological Seminary, Chicago, Illinois.

John W. Coakley is L. Russell Feakes professor of church history and director of the Center for Reformed Church Studies at New Brunswick Theological Seminary, New Brunswick, New Jersey.

Paul R. Fries is academic dean and professor of theology at New Brunswick Theological Seminary, New Brunswick, New Jersey.

Douglas Fromm is minister of Upper Ridgewood Community Church, Ridgewood, New Jersey, and associate for ecumenical relations in the office of the general secretary of the Reformed Church in America.

Wesley Granberg-Michaelson is general secretary of the Reformed Church in America.

Herman Harmelink III is ecumenical officer of the International Council of Community Churches and retired minister of the Reformed Church of Poughkeepsie, New York.

Dale T. Irvin is professor of world Christianity at New York Theological Seminary.

Allan Janssen is minister of the Community Church of Glen Rock, New Jersey.

Lynn Japinga is associate professor of religion at Hope College, Holland, Michigan.

Gregg A. Mast is minister of First Church in Albany, New York.

David Melvin is general manager of Total Living Network Interactive and former vice president of the National Association of Evangelicals.

Dennis Tamburello, O.F.M. is professor of religious studies at Siena College, Loudonville, New York.

Introduction

John W. Coakley

The twentieth century saw the birth of the modern ecumenical movement. In its first several decades, which straddled the founding of the World Council of Churches in 1948, the movement's prevailing visions of Christian unity appeared to imply the necessity that Christian diversity would fade. But by the end of the century the tendency was rather to accept, even to celebrate, the diversity of Christian traditions and churches and to envision a unity that would consist instead in their profound and necessary interdependence. As the present WCC general secretary, Konrad Raiser, has written, "Relations with other churches as members of the ecumenical household or in conciliar fellowship belong inalienably to the *esse* of the church. No church can be church in the full meaning of the word apart from the other churches."[1]

The idea of Christian unity as interdependence within diversity informs this volume of essays. The essays explore the relationships between the churches of the Reformed tradition (understood here broadly as that tradition with roots in the faith and practice of the Reformation of the South German and Swiss cities of the sixteenth century, including most famously Geneva[2]) and the churches of other Christian traditions. These

---

1   Konrad Raiser, *Ecumenism in Transition: A Paradigm Shift in the Ecumenical Movement?* (Geneva: World Council of Churches, 1991), 116. See also Dale T. Irvin, *Hearing Many Voices: Dialogue and Diversity in the Ecumenical Movement* (Lanham: University Press of America, 1993).

2   The Reformed tradition is otherwise notoriously hard to define or characterize. Two attempts to discern its cohesion are: M. Eugene Osterhaven, *The Spirit of the Reformed*

relationships are each distinctive in the issues they raise, and the picture of ecumenism here is characterized by anything but a fading of diversity. On the other hand, the essays also convey collectively a sense of the necessity of these relationships—a sense that the lot of the Reformed churches is inevitably cast with that of other Christian traditions and that without those relationships, in their very complexity, Reformed churches would not know themselves or be able to fulfill their mission.

More than half of the essays here—seven of the thirteen—focus more narrowly upon the ecumenical experience of one particular church, the Reformed Church in America (RCA), which traces its history to the colonial era in America and has roots in the Reformed Church of the Netherlands.[3] Those essays consider in some detail the RCA's ecumenical relationships in recent years; however, they are intended not merely as an exploration of denominational history but also as a sort of collective case study, an exploration of the broader issues of Reformed ecumenism as evidenced within the particular historical experience of one Reformed church.

This is not the first published study of ecumenism with a focus on the RCA. A third of a century ago, the scholar and pastor, Herman Harmelink, wrote *Ecumenism and the Reformed Church*, which appeared in print as the first volume in the Historical Series of the Reformed Church in America, of which the present volume is the forty-first. In that study, Harmelink surveyed the long history of attempts to merge the RCA with other churches. In every case, Harmelink showed, those attempts had not succeeded; typically the church had displayed, as he put it, an "ecumenical-separatist split personality[4]." Yet even though mergers had remained elusive, Harmelink's book demonstrated that the issues attending them had been so extraordinarily important to the RCA that to account for these was almost to write a general history of the denomination.

Tradition (Grand Rapids: Eerdmans, 1970) and John Leith, *An Introduction to the Reformed Tradition* (Atlanta: John Knox Press, 1977). See also Jean-Jacques Bauswein and Lukas Vischer, *The Reformed Family Worldwide: A Survey of Reformed Churches, Theological Schools and International Organizations* (Grand Rapids: Eerdmans, 1999), and Hendrik Vroom, "On Being Reformed," in *Reformed and Ecumenical*, ed. C. Lienemann-Perrin, *et al.* (Amsterdam: Rodopi, 2000), 153-69.

3   Readers unfamiliar with the RCA may find a succinct account of its history by Elton J. Bruins in Daniel G. Reid, *et al.*, eds., *Dictionary of Christianity in America* (Downers Grove, Ill.: InterVarsity Press, 1990), 986.

4   Herman Harmelink III, *Ecumenism and the Reformed Church* (Grand Rapids: Eerdmans, 1968), 94.

Harmelink's book stands, in retrospect, as a kind of a valedictory for the passing of ecumenism as that term was widely understood in the mid-twentieth century—as a movement toward merger or organic union among churches, and in that sense a movement away from diversity. Although the grand intra-communion mergers that created the Presbyterian Church (U.S.A.) in 1983 and the Evangelical Lutheran Church in America in 1987 were still in the future when Harmelink wrote, idealistic hopes for more ambitious organic unions—such as had motivated churches of divergent polities to form the United Church of Christ in 1957, or to formulate the heady union visions of the Consultation on Church Union—were disappearing fast along with other optimistic dreams and convictions of the post-World War II religious boom. In the RCA itself, the proposal for union with the southern Presbyterian Church (PCUS), which was pending at the time *Ecumenism and the Reformed Church* appeared and which failed to win the necessary margin of approval by RCA classes in 1968-69, was the last such proposal that the RCA has seriously considered.

So no one talks about merger anymore. Still, ecumenism, if we understand the term to refer to efforts toward deepening the relationships between Christian communions, has remained at least as important an item on the RCA's, and other churches', agendas in the intervening years as it was in 1968. The *Ecumenical Mandate* approved by the General Synod in 1996 suggests a complex picture of RCA ecumenism in which ecumenical relationships are pursued at many levels in many ways— through an array of cooperative mission projects with other churches, through the conciliar bodies such as the WCC and the National Council of Churches, and through various long-term inter-communion dialogues, some of which are aimed at finding ways for churches to enter "full pulpit and table fellowship" with each other.[5] It is exactly from such ecumenical relationships that many of the leading controversies in the denomination in recent years have emerged, such as the discussions about the church's stance toward the Dutch Reformed Church in South Africa during the years of Apartheid, about its reception of Canadian congregations who had left the United Church of Canada and, more recently, about its

5   *An Ecumenical Mandate for the Reformed Church in America* (Grand Rapids: RCA Distribution Center, n.d.). The text also appears in *Minutes of the General Synod, RCA,* 1995, 174-86.

rapport with the United Church of Christ in the context of the Lutheran/ Reformed Formula of Agreement.[6]

In view of this changed but highly charged ecumenical situation, the time has seemed ripe for a "new Harmelink," a new attempt, that is, to take stock of "ecumenism and the Reformed Church." The focus is a little wider than Harmelink's, in the sense that, as I have suggested already, the essays collectively examine not only the RCA but the broader Reformed tradition as well. Also the title may raise an eyebrow or two in the RCA. The more familiar translations of the Dutch motto inscribed on the denomination's seal, "*Eendracht maakt Macht*," construe *eendracht* as "union" or "unity."[7] Yet whereas those English words can connote a numerical unity, a disappearance of the many into the one, the Dutch word cannot. It implies the sort of unity achieved by efforts that are exerted in the same direction, for the same ends, and yet remain implicitly discrete.[8] The word "concord," as an alternative to "union" or "unity," respects that discreteness, while at the same time not excluding a sense of a unity that is potentially deep and significant, even though not numerical. To assert that, in this sense, "concord makes strength," may not only better catch the nuance of the Dutch phrase than the more familiar translation, but it also expresses the current ecumenism at its most hopeful.

The collection of essays is in three parts. The essays in part one provide historical and theological perspectives on the current landscape of Reformed relationships with other traditions. Here Herman Harmelink surveys current ecumenical trends in the light of his previous work, and Lynn Japinga makes a sustained analysis of two debates over merger

---

6   On South Africa, see Jack Klunder, "A History of Synodical Opposition to the Heresy of Apartheid," in *Servant Gladly: Essays in Honor of John W. Beardslee III*, ed. Jack D. Klunder and Russell L. Gasero (Grand Rapids: Eerdmans, 1989), 49-72; on the reception of the Canadian congregations, see John Stapert, "Migrating UCC [United Church of Canada] Churches Swell RCA Ranks in Canada," *Church Herald* 48 no. 5 (May 1991):43-45, and anon., "Canada and the Right to Know," *Church Herald* 48 no. 7 (July/August 1991):10-11; on the United Church of Christ and the Formula of Agreement, see Douglas Fromm's essay in chapter 5 of this volume.

7   The motto is "a free rendering of '*Concordia res parvae crescunt*' found upon medals and coins struck to commemorate the [16th-century] Union of the States of the Netherlands." Edward T. Corwin, *A Digest of Constitutional and Synodical Legislation of the Reformed Church in America* (New York: Board of Publication of the Reformed Church in America, 1906), 253.

8   I thank Okke Postma for calling attention to this point.

proposals in the post-World War II period to consider the roots of an enduring "counter-ecumenism" within the RCA. Then Karel Blei and Paul Fries consider ecumenical themes from the standpoint of the classic Reformed doctrinal documents of the Reformation period, in both cases finding Christian unity to be envisioned there both in terms of churches and in terms of believers—views that are not identical and that, together, create a certain tension within the tradition.

The essays in part two, the longest section of the book, consider four different areas of Reformed encounter with other communions and traditions. First, Douglas Fromm surveys the effect of the Reformed/Lutheran Formula of Agreement of 1998 within the RCA, which suggests that the Formula has opened the door less to an ongoing theological encounter between the Reformed and Lutheran traditions than to a pragmatic sense of cooperation at various levels of church life. Second, three essays reflect on the state of relations between the Reformed and Roman Catholic traditions: the Franciscan scholar Dennis Tamburello discusses the implications of *Dominus Iesus*, the recent controversial statement from the Vatican's Congregation for the Doctrine of the Faith; Anna Case-Winters considers what contributions the Reformed tradition might make to the recent Lutheran/Roman Catholic accords on the doctrine of Justification; and Gregg Mast argues that the rise of Christianity in parts of the world where culture was not shaped by the sixteenth-century Reformation may help the worldwide church to heal the persistent Reformation divisions by transcending them. Third, Karel Blei explores both the promise and the difficulties of the bilateral dialogues between the Reformed and Eastern Orthodox churches, and in particular the questions these dialogues raise about the relation between tradition and the modern world. Finally, Allan Janssen and David Melvin examine an ecumenical issue of a rather different sort, namely the relation between the Reformed and Evangelical traditions; here it is a matter of significantly overlapping, rather than mutually exclusive, traditions—especially from the standpoint of the RCA—and yet, at certain points, no less problematic for that.

The two essays in part three consider the future of ecumenism. Here Dale Irvin explains the plan now being bruited for a conference in 2004 to reformulate the terms of the Faith and Order Movement—one of the major formative elements of the twentieth-century ecumenical movement—on terms that, as Irvin says, would not operate from the metaphor of gathering at a common table, but rather would acknowledge "the need for each group to learn how to sit at the tables of others," thus attempting to take better account of the real diversity of Christian witness. Wesley Granberg-Michaelson also points to that diversity, in the essay that concludes our volume, with illustrations of how, in the context of a rapidly growing worldwide Christianity, old ecumenical strategies often seem irrelevant.

Although these essays argue a variety of points from a variety of perspectives, some recurring themes help tie the essays to one another. I point to three of these.

One theme to be found in several of the essays is that of the ecumenical implications of the patterns of growth in the Christian movement worldwide. In the southern hemisphere, especially in Asia and Latin America, but even in our country, there has been explosive growth precisely among Pentecostal and other churches which have little connection to, or interest in, the conciliar movements and bilateral conversations that served to focus the ecumenism of the twentieth century. As Granberg-Michaelson, Mast, and Irvin all imply in their essays, whatever the future of those older movements and conversations may be, it is imperative that we pursue new and different approaches— perhaps, as Granberg-Michaelson suggests, building upon an affirmation of the baptism common to most Christians.

A second theme is tied to, although perhaps also in some tension with, the first: the importance of a strong awareness of the witness of our own Reformed tradition—the importance, that is, of looking to the past and not only to the future. In the current situation in America in which, as the work of Robert Wuthnow and others has shown, Christians' sense of identification with particular denominational traditions has been diminishing drastically, the resources of those traditions constitute indispensable resources for finding a place to stand, a place from which to observe, and speak with, and reach out to, other Christians.[9] Thus the essays here by Blei, Fries, Case-Winters, and Janssen, by bringing the Reformed confessions and other elements of the Reformed tradition to bear upon the issues that currently face us, serve as reminders of the

---

9   Robert Wuthnow, *The Restructuring of American Religion* (Princeton: Princeton University Press, 1988).

particularity of our own tradition without which, whatever new ecumenical paths we find ourselves taking, we will not know who we are.

The third and final theme I want to point out suggests a different, but no less interesting, sort of reflection. This is the theme of the significance of ecumenical issues for the life we share with the other members of our own church. As the essays of Japinga, Tamburello, Harmelink, and Janssen make especially clear, a church's discussion of its external relationships may very well also stand as a (sometimes unacknowledged) discussion of its internal relationships—as, for example, in Japinga's accounts of the merger controversies of the 1950s and 1960s, of which she comments that "it was easier to fight over the relative orthodoxy of another group when the real issue was lack of trust of the others in one's own group." Much more recently, no participant in General Synod debates of the last few years about the RCA's relationship with the United Church of Christ, in which the beliefs and inclinations of that church were ostensibly at issue, can doubt that we who took part in the debates were also making an issue of each other's beliefs and inclinations, even though we seldom said so directly. The encounter with other traditions, it would seem, reaches deeply into our own selves precisely in our identity as members of our own tradition, whether we wish it to or not—a perhaps not entirely welcome sign that ecumenical relationships are indeed of the essence of the church.

It was, of course, exactly because ecumenism reaches so deeply into us that, as I noted above, Herman Harmelink's classic history of RCA ecumenism could almost function as a history of the RCA itself. Even though the present volume offers a collection of perspectives rather than a "history" in the sense implied by a single-author narrative, still that same deep reach of ecumenism also makes this volume a witness to matters that are not just of interest to the Reformed tradition but evidently lie at its very heart.

1

Ecumenism and the Reformed Church Revisited

Herman Harmelink

I have been asked to revisit the matter of ecumenism and the Reformed Church, some thirty-four years after my book by that title was published as the first volume in the Historical Series of the Reformed Church in America.[1] Some readers may recall that at that time the Reformed Church was considering union with the Presbyterian Church in the United States, then the southern branch of our sister church. The book was published at the beginning of the year during which the classes of the Reformed Church and the presbyteries of the Presbyterian Church were to vote on the proposed union. At the conclusion of the book, I went out on a limb by making a few predictions. Was it Mark Twain who said, "Never prophesy, especially about the future"? Actually I did not predict the success or failure of the vote, though I knew it would be unlikely that many of the western classes of the Reformed Church would vote for union. I had not imagined that *every* classis in the West would vote against it, thereby assuring its failure even though it was approved by every eastern classis and by the Presbyterians.

---

1 Herman Harmelink III, *Ecumenism and the Reformed Church* (Grand Rapids: Eerdmans, 1968).

1

Rather than making out-and-out predictions, I sketched three possible scenarios for the future, depending on whether the union with the Presbyterian Church in the U.S. were approved or not. Scenario I, the one I preferred at the time, would have been for the Reformed Church to join forces with the Presbyterians.[2] It seemed to me that the Reformed Church would lose nothing, and would gain a great deal, by being part of a larger and stronger branch of the Reformed-Presbyterian family. As we all now know, that did not happen, which leaves Scenarios II and III.

Scenario II was that there would be a division between the eastern, ecumenical, branch of the Reformed Church and the western, more conservative, branch of the church.[3] This nearly happened at the General Synod of 1969, after the announcement that the Plan of Union had been defeated. Harold Schut, a former president of the General Synod, made a motion at that synod that the church be divided into two parts, much as Scenario II had pictured.[4] This would have freed eastern congregations, classes, and synods to join the Presbyterian Church, and the western congregations to continue a separate existence or to amalgamate with the Christian Reformed Church or some other communion of conservative Calvinists.[5] As we all now know, that also did not happen.

That leaves Scenario III: maintenance of the status quo,[6] which in fact is what happened, except that the status quo never stands still. At the time I was president of the Synod of New Jersey, in 1969, we had 46,856 members, and there were 62,950 members in New

---

2   Ibid, 88.
3   Ibid.
4   *Minutes of the General Synod,* 1969, 200-204.
5   That the Christian Reformed Church never became a candidate to be considered for a church union was due to its suspicion of the Reformed Church's orthodoxy. In the last decade, the denomination has lost about fifty thousand members over the issue of ordination of women, a matter settled affirmatively in the Reformed Church a generation ago.
6   Harmelink, *Ecumenism,* 88.

York State in the synods of New York and Albany.[7] In the latest statistics, the three eastern synods have a combined membership of 47,935, or substantially less than half of what they had three decades ago.[8] More significant for the future of ecumenical relations is the fact that the eastern synods now make up about 25 percent of the total membership, in contrast to the 50 percent they made up thirty years ago. If church union was not possible with 50 percent of the total membership, because it needed to be approved by two-thirds of the classes, it is far more remote when the 50 percent favorable to church union has declined to 25 percent of the whole.

There is another reason why proposals for church union have not arisen within the Reformed Church over the past thirty years. Church unions such as were frequent during the first three-quarters of the twentieth century have now gone out of fashion. In large part this is due to disillusionment with the effectiveness of denominational structures. If the existing structures of two denominations are inefficient or unproductive, putting them together might merely compound the inefficiencies. Localism and congregationalism now engage most parishes more than the broader view, and if this makes them effective in local mission, it would seem to be a good fault. More frequently, though, the concentration on parish affairs is related to a struggle for survival in the face of declining institutional church life.

Certainly the emphasis in ecumenism in recent decades, as a result of bilateral and multilateral conversations, has been on full communion, rather than outright union. The Evangelical Lutheran Church in America has played a major role in this development. As one of the largest Protestant denominations in the United States, the Evangelical Lutheran Church today deserves, more than does the Episcopal Church, the title of "bridge church." Episcopalians used to see their church as the bridge between Protestants and Roman Catholics, but it often seems to be a bridge connected at

7 *Minutes of the General Synod,* 1969, Appendix 2, p. 62.
8 *Minutes of the General Synod,* 2000, Directory, 132-33.

neither end.[9] The Lutherans have established full communion with the three Reformed churches in the United States,[10] a development only about two centuries behind Lutheran and Reformed churches in Germany, [11] and even behind the Dutch Protestant churches. Visiting our ancestral Dutch village a few weeks ago, I was interested to see that the church there is no longer called the Dutch Reformed Church, but instead "The United Protestant Church."[12] The Lutherans in America have also established full communion with the Episcopal Church and the Moravian Church. In addition, and this may be the most significant ecumenical development of all, they have reached an agreed statement on the doctrine of justification by faith with the Roman Catholic Church.

It remains to be seen, of course, how much effect these formulae of agreement on full communion and on justification by faith will have in the communions and in the church at large. Father Burke of the Catholic University in Washington once told me of his astonishment at discovering that indulgences were still being sold in Spain. "Don't the Spanish realize that indulgences were abolished at the Council of Trent?" he asked. "Oh, yes," came the reply, "but those decrees have never been promulgated in Spain." It isn't only

---

[9] The Episcopal Church cannot fully accept Protestant churches unless those churches accept the Episcopal definition of apostolic succession as one of institutional continuity rather than continuity of apostolic faith; the Roman Catholic Church cannot fully accept the Episcopal Church because of its ordination of women. In 1896 the Roman Catholic Church declared Anglican orders "invalid," and it has not altered that position.

[10] The Presbyterian Church (USA), the Reformed Church in America, and the United Church of Christ. See the essay in this volume by Douglas Fromm.

[11] The Evangelische Kirche in Deutschland (Protestant Church in Germany) came into being at the end of World War II, but its largest constituent, the Evangelical Church of the Union, was formed between the Lutheran and Reformed Churches in Prussia in 1817. It and other Union churches make up half of the EkiD. See Heinz Brunotte, *The Evangelical Church in Germany* (Hanover: Verlag des Amtsblattes der Evangelischen Kirche, 1962).

[12] Comprising the *Nederlandse Hervormde Kerk*, the *GereformeerdeKerken in Nederland*, and the Evangelical Lutherans.

those decrees have never been promulgated in Spain." It isn't only the Roman Catholic Church that knows how to make a dead letter out of an action that lacks popular support.

Perhaps the most remarkable ecumenical phenomenon in the United States today is the renewed interest on the part of nine communions in the Consultation on Church Union (COCU). The death of this movement was both predicted and announced on many occasions during the more than forty years it has been in existence. Originally, Eugene Carson Blake of the Presbyterian Church called for four churches to take the initiative in calling a consultation, looking towards the union of churches which would produce one American Protestant Church, truly catholic, truly evangelical, truly reformed. As many as twelve denominations have been a part of the consultation, but because unions have occurred within the COCU, the membership now stands at nine.[13] All nine of these communions have voted to come together in an inaugural celebration in January of 2002 in Memphis, bringing into being a new organization called Churches Uniting in Christ. This organization will not be a church union along traditional lines, because the different communions will retain their uniqueness and much of their individuality, but the churches are committing themselves to regularly scheduled services of the Eucharist; joint participation in baptisms, confirmations, and ordinations; and joint participation in local and regional mission. There will also be a commitment to achieve recognition and reconciliation of ministries by the year 2007. The nine bodies include three predominantly African-American Methodist churches and the United Methodist Church, as well as the Disciples of Christ, the Episcopal Church, the International Council of Community Churches, the Presbyterian Church, and the United Church of Christ. In addition, the Evangelical Lutheran Church, the American Baptists, and the Moravians have

---

[13] The Reformed Church failed twice, once by ten votes and another time by two votes, to become a member of COCU. *Minutes of the General Synod*, 1967, 266-67; 1972, 105-106. It has from time to time participated as an observer.

accepted a role which goes beyond observer status, and which is called "Partner in Mission and Witness."

The other major ecumenical endeavors carried over from the twentieth century are the conciliar ones—the World Council of Churches, the National Council of the Churches of Christ in the USA, and state and local councils of churches or interfaith councils. Both the World and National councils grew out of the missionary concern that has always challenged ecumenical activists: to reveal the essential unity of the church and the Christian faith so that the world may see this unity and believe. Both councils have been working to make the faith vivid in action—helping those who need help anywhere in the world. If one had to classify councils of churches, one could say that the weight of activity falls on the "life and work" side of the equation rather than on the "faith and order" side. Both councils have come under heavy criticism at times by outsiders who believe that any concern for the less privileged is evidence of leftist or communist tendencies, overlooking the bias in favor of the poor throughout the Scriptures and in much of the church's history. Today both the World and National councils are under heavy financial pressure. In the World Council, it is due in large part to the reduced contribution of the German churches, where many people opt out of the church tax.[14] In the United States, the National Council has suffered from a push-and-pull between Church World Service, the relief arm of the church, which has most of the money, and the central administration, which needs a portion of Church World Service monies to maintain the overall organization.

At present there is a great deal of discussion about extending the ecumenical table by trying to devise a new ecumenical structure that could include, along with the National Council members, the Roman Catholic Church, conservative evangelicals, and pentecostals.[15] Some believe that this effort is a result of financial

[14] The church tax represents 1 percent of a person's income tax.
[15] See the essay in this volume by Dale Irvin.

pressures on the part of the National Council, but I believe the desire goes much deeper than that. Roman Catholics make up a quarter of the nation's population, and roughly half of the Christian population of America. I am not, however, optimistic that this broader coalition will be achieved easily, if at all. Cardinal Ratzinger's recent document, *Dominus Iesus,* now an official statement from the Vatican, says that there is only one true church, and all others are defective.[16] Even if there was a degree of mistranslation of the document into English, it seems to have been couched in undiplomatic and unecumenical language, hardly a signal of desire for closer relations between Rome and the other churches. And the self-described "conservative evangelicals" are, somewhat similarly, difficult to engage in ecumenical relations because of their decentralized style of organization and an abiding suspicion on their part that mainline churches are "liberal" and therefore not fully or adequately Christian.

Will the National Council of Churches survive its present stresses? I believe it will, because, as someone has said, if it disappeared we would have to start another one. The churches have grown used to working together, and many people count on the National Council to be a national voice for the churches. Whether it will survive in its present form, even if the Roman Catholics and conservative evangelicals do not ally themselves with it, is another question. Nine member churches will soon belong to Churches Uniting in Christ, with three other mainline churches aligned with them as Partners in Mission and Witness.[17] Besides those twelve churches, there is in the National Council a large Eastern Orthodox grouping of eleven communions,[18] a large grouping of seven communions with

---

16 See the essays in this volume by Karel Blei and Dennis Tamburello.

17 The nine COCU churches have a membership of nearly 21 million; with the three partners, a total of nearly 28 million of the National Council's 45 million. Source: *The World Almanac and Book of Facts 2001* (Mahway, N.J.: World Almanac Books, 2001), 689-90.

18 These churches have a membership of 3,785,780. Source: ibid.

dominant memberships of particular race or ethnicity,[19] and then the following four: the Church of the Brethren, the Quakers, the Swedenborgians, and the Reformed Church in America.[20] It will be natural and inevitable that many decisions will be taken by Churches Uniting in Christ, giving the remaining groups a secondary level of membership in the council.

A question of deeper concern for many readers might be whether the Reformed Church in America will survive. I have recently read Jonathan Israel's wonderful book, *The Dutch Republic: Its Rise, Greatness and Fall*.[21] Israel traces the origins of the republic in the counties of the lowlands ruled by Burgundy in the fifteenth century, through the battle for independence from the Hapsburgs, the battles with England and alliances with them, to the ultimate decline of the republic and its absorption into the French Empire under Napoleon. Is a similar fate in store for the Dutch Reformed church?

I do not think so. Many years ago, after having attended a meeting of the U.S. Conference of the World Council of Churches at Buck Hill Falls, I was standing on the station platform waiting for the train back to New York. I became engaged in conversation with an Oriental gentleman who'd also been at the conference. I asked him what church he was from, and he said, "The Chinese Christian Church of Indonesia." "Just what is that, actually?" I asked him, and he said, "Well, actually, it's Dutch Reformed." I said, "You mean there is a Chinese-speaking Dutch Reformed Church in Indonesia?" He allowed how that was so, and then he asked the name of my church. When I said, "The Reformed Church in America," he said, "Well, what is that, actually?" And I responded, "Dutch Reformed." "You mean there's an English-speaking Dutch Reformed Church in America?" he asked. I had long been aware of the staying power of the Dutch Reformed, having been married in the mother of all

---

[19] These churches have a membership of 13,232,968. Source: ibid.
[20] These churches have a membership of 365,365. Source: ibid.
[21] New York: Oxford University Press, 1995.

Dutch Reformed churches (Austin Friars in London, which was founded in 1550).[22] But after the conversation with the Chinese gentleman, one thing became crystal clear to me: even if Christianity should perish from the earth, there would still be a Dutch Reformed church!

---

[22] The oldest Dutch Reformed church in the world is in London because it was not permitted to be Protestant in Spanish-ruled Holland, so Dutch Protestant refugees were given the former Augustinian monastery in London by King Edward VI.

2

On Second Thought: A Hesitant History of Ecumenism in the Reformed Church in America

Lynn Japinga

Most of the essays in this book describe successful moments in the ecumenical history of the Reformed Church in America (RCA) or hopeful prospects for the future. This essay explores what might be called "counterecumenism," or the reasons for the RCA's reluctance to enter into unions with other churches. Herman Harmelink has described many of these failed merger attempts in his study of the history of RCA ecumenism.[1] In this essay, I will examine two attempted mergers: with the United Presbyterian Church in North America in 1949-1950 and with the Presbyterian Church in the United States (southern) in 1968-1969.

Throughout most of its history, the RCA has cooperated with other denominations in missionary work and in ecumenical councils, recognizing that the gospel was rightly preached in other denominations. Perhaps the strongest statement of RCA commitment to the slogan, "In concord there is strength," appears in a policy statement adopted by the General Synod in 1966 entitled, "The Unity We Seek to Manifest." After claiming that God calls

---

[1] Herman Harmelink III, *Ecumenism and the Reformed Church* (Grand Rapids: Eerdmans, 1968).

forth the one Church to proclaim the gospel, the statement continues with this ringing endorsement of unity:

> In obedience to this divine revelation we of the Reformed Church in America resolve to manifest the God-given unity of the Church by working to overcome our divisions. The ways and means to unity are not always known. The goal of unity is a venture of faith. Therefore, trusting in the Holy Spirit for guidance, we shall be open to His counsel, willing to converse with any church, ready to cooperate with all Christians, committed to participate in councils of churches on all levels, prepared to merge with any church when it is clearly the will of God, eager to heal the brokenness of the Body of Christ in all ways made known to us, until all are one, so that the world may know that the Father has sent the Son as Saviour and Lord.[2]

A genuine commitment to this statement might have led to one or two mergers, full participation in the Consultation on Church Union (COCU), and an enthusiastic commitment to the National and World Councils of Churches. The reality, however, has not quite lived up to the ideal.

Theoretically, the Reformed Church supports ecumenism, but its actions tell a more complicated story. The denomination has been willing to converse, form committees, send people to meetings, and engage in hours and months and years of talk but never to unite with another body. To use a sexist but popular metaphor, the church seems willing to flirt with any suitor, to exclaim how much she has in common with the suitor and how much she likes him, and to plan for marriage, only to dump the poor fellow unceremoniously when he is already dressed in his tuxedo. What were the reasons for such hesitance? Why was there such a gap between the initial yes and the final no?

---

2 *Minutes of the General Synod, RCA* (hereafter, *Minutes*), 1965, 295.

Harmelink argues that the RCA failed to complete merger discussions primarily because of the provincialism and conservatism of midwestern members, who opposed merger not for theological reasons but because of social and cultural preferences resulting from their secessionist history and spirit. These nontheological factors are significant, but there are also theological reasons that explain the Midwest's reluctance to merge. Letters to the editor in the *Church Herald*, articles published by various groups of laymen and clergy, and the correspondence collected by Norman Thomas and Marion DeVelder on the subject demonstrate a deep sense of fear. Many conservatives did not simply dislike the idea of merger, they were profoundly afraid of it. They used words like "sabotage," "sterility," and "bankruptcy." They spoke of writing an obituary for the Reformed Church and the historic Christian faith. One author argued that merger would "emasculate the true Biblical faith."[3] They feared being taken over, swallowed up, or amalgamated and thereby losing their identity, heritage, and voice. Most of all, perhaps, they feared the slippery slope. They were convinced that merging with one of these small Presbyterian groups would lead to bigger and far more horrible things, first the northern Presbyterians, then COCU, then Rome, and finally the apostate church of the Antichrist. Thirty years later, such fears may seem a bit excessive, especially since we know how little has happened in COCU, but their fear must be taken seriously if we are to understand what made people in the Midwest so hesitant about mergers.

The failure of the two mergers cannot simply be attributed to midwestern paranoia. The social contexts of eastern and midwestern churches were significantly different in the post-World War II decades. The following somewhat exaggerated scenario may help illustrate the respective cultural contexts.[4]

3   Harris VerKaik, letter to the editor, *Church Herald*, 11 August 1967, 23.
4   The generalizations, "midwestern" and "eastern," are commonly used to describe theological and ecclesiastical viewpoints in the RCA, but many exceptions can be found. Generally, midwestern churches were more theologically conservative and less interested in ecumenism, but there were

John and Mary Smith are members of the Levittown Community Church in New York in 1966. They moved to New York from a suburb of Chicago, where they had been members of a Presbyterian church. Their best friends are Peter and Peggy Jones, who had transferred their membership recently from a Southern Presbyterian church in Atlanta. All four of them liked the congregation, but they had never heard of the Reformed Church in America. After trying unsuccessfully to explain, the pastor told them the RCA was a Dutch version of Presbyterian. But it didn't matter all that much. Their potluck group included a Methodist, two Baptists, a Catholic, and a Jewish-Episcopalian couple. When they got together they talked about the school system, the church youth group, and the New York Jets.

Eight hundred miles away in western Michigan, Bill and Connie Dykstra attend the Hudsonville Reformed Church in which Bill grew up and which several of his family members also attend. The couple met while attending Hope College. Connie was from the Second Reformed Church in Hamilton. Three of her uncles were Reformed Church ministers, and her cousin was a missionary in the Middle East. Their Bible study group included six people from Hudsonville, a woman from Jersey City who had met her husband at Hope, and two people from Grand Rapids who had a mixed marriage (the husband having been Christian Reformed). When they got together they discussed the authority of Scripture, the historicity of Adam, and those eastern churches that wanted to ordain women as elders.

These scenarios are obviously overstated caricatures, and yet they help illustrate an important dimension of RCA ecumenism. John Smith and Bill Dykstra might have been elder delegates to their respective classes in the winter of 1969, when the RCA voted

churches, pastors, and laypeople in the Midwest that were more ecumenical. Similarly, the eastern churches tended to be somewhat more theologically liberal and interested in ecumenism, but there were exceptions. It should also be noted that "more liberal" in the RCA is still moderate or even conservative on the theological spectrum of American religion.

whether to merge with the Southern Presbyterian Church. John might have said, "Yes, of course we should merge. I don't see any real difference between the two and it would strengthen our witness in the city." Bill might have said, "No, we don't know them, and why would we want to risk losing our family feeling by getting bigger?" Attitudes toward ecumenism in the RCA, whether enthusiastic or hesitant, have a great deal to do with cultural and social context, but a decision about merger is also a theological decision. This paper will explore both the cultural and the theological factors that led Reformed Church members to such differing views of ecumenical responsibility.

The United Presbyterian Church in North America

In 1945 the General Synod voted to hold merger discussions with the United Presbyterian Church in North America (UPC). The church was a little larger than the RCA, doctrinally similar, and located primarily in Pennsylvania and Ohio. Initial response in the Reformed Church was very favorable, even in the Midwest. In the spring of 1946, Louis Benes, the new editor of the *Church Herald*, wrote that the proposal represented a middle ground between joining with everyone and joining with no one. The two denominations had a great deal in common, he said, and if we are one in Christ, what business do we have staying apart? The RCA should not be sentimental about its past or interested only in its own people. A month later, Benes pointed out that merger would help the RCA be more efficient and expand in major cities where it lacked a presence.[5]

By the 1946 meeting of the General Synod, a joint committee from the two denominations had determined that their doctrine and polity were generally uniform. The committee was directed to draft a Plan of Union to distribute in the fall of 1946. The synod also approved plans for fellowship and pulpit exchanges between the

5   Louis Benes, editorial, "Church Union," *Church Herald*, 26 April 1946, 5; "A Strategy for the Reformed Church," 24 May 1946, 5.

two churches. The *Church Herald* helped vacationing ministers exchange pulpits and ran articles showing the two churches' many similarities. The two denominations appeared to be rushing pellmell to the altar.

Then Benes invited letters to the editor. Both lay people and clergy offered a variety of reasons against the merger: Merger with the Christian Reformed Church was more logical. The RCA's heritage was unique and precious and needed to be preserved. Merger allowed more room for liberalism. The RCA did not need to be bigger. The UPC did not encourage catechetical instruction and therefore merger could not be a step forward. The fear of loss is best captured in the words of one lay person: "The way our church feels, many members will leave the church. I'm sure it will create more hot heads than warm hearts....We have belonged to the Reformed Church all our lives. The Reformed Church has gotten along very well, and we have peace in our fellowship, while union might bring strife."[6] These writers did not object to the UPC so much as grieve what the RCA might lose in a merger.

The RCA did not have to wait for union to bring strife. Conflict came in the wake of what was known as the "Blast from Bast," a series of letters and pamphlets written by Henry Bast, a pastor in Grand Rapids, Michigan. Bast accused New Brunswick Seminary, the Board of Foreign Missions, and eastern churches in general of liberalism and lack of spiritual vitality. The Midwest gave most of the money, he claimed, but the East had all the power. Eastern members controlled the boards and made the decisions, even though they did not have enough spiritual commitment to contribute their fair share.

Bast's critique let loose a flood of criticism of both the Federal Council of Churches (FCC) and the United Presbyterian Church. Membership in the FCC, for example, had always been a point of

---

6 Herman De Vries, letter to the editor, *Church Herald*, 25 October 1946, 6. See also Paul Wezeman, letter, 25 October 1946, 6, and G.H. Hospers, letter, 8 November 1946.

tension, but after much discussion in the early 1930s, there had only been a few overtures opposed to the FCC. In 1947, after Bast's Blast, there were nine overtures against, and seven for, continued membership. Much of the criticism revolved around alleged liberalism in the council and its minimalist approach to theology. People feared that the FCC would corrupt the Reformed Church, and they encouraged the RCA to preserve its purity and its faith by separating from this dangerous group.

Similar suspicion and criticism were directed to the United Presbyterian Church. It was more difficult to find liberalism in the UPC, as its doctrine and ethos were very similar to the RCA. The UPC was conservative, confessional, Reformed yet somewhat pietistic, and deeply committed to the gospel. However, RCA critics found that UPC laypeople were not required to subscribe to the confessions, which seemed to open the door to liberalism. The UPC also said that Scripture was *an* infallible rule rather than *the* infallible rule as the RCA claimed to believe, and this distinction caused critics to conclude that the UPC did not hold the Bible in sufficiently high regard. Many writers simply used innuendo and vague generalizations to say that a merger would be the beginning of the end of Reformed orthodoxy.

It was even more common, however, to argue for the value of RCA identity and to bemoan the potential loss of name, status, and history. Jerome DeJong feared the RCA would lose its doctrinal distinctiveness and become like other churches that had no more doctrine than vague advice to love the neighbor. Harry Hager believed that the newly merged church would not continue the emphasis on the beloved (at least in the Midwest) Sunday evening service and Heidelberg Catechism. He was also appalled to discover that most of the UPC colleges allowed dancing, and one had a smoking lounge for its women students.[7] It was clear to him that

---

7   Jerome DeJong, letter to the editor, *Church Herald*, 7 February 1947, 8; Harry Hager, "Shall We Be Reformed or Presbyterian?" 2 December 1949, 12-13, 23.

merger would lower the moral standards in the RCA. Merger also threatened to expand the bureaucratic machinery that many midwesterners already resented. Critics feared that instead of sending out more missionaries and starting new congregations, the new denomination would be top heavy, unwieldy, and unresponsive to its people.

Several authors feared that merger with the UPC would lead to a future merger with the northern Presbyterians. Harri Zegerius pointed out that Presbyterians often talked about unions with their extended "family," and he warned, "When you marry a girl you may not necessarily want to marry the relatives."[8] He and other conservatives in the RCA felt that the northern Presbyterians had become hopelessly liberal. They were not opposed to the UPC itself, but to a denomination with which it might eventually merge. Some feared that the slippery slope of merger would not end with the Presbyterians. Opponents of merger pointed out that if denominations were a sign of brokenness and sin, as many ecumenists argued, then the logical conclusion was to abolish denominations altogether and return to Rome. Opposition to Catholics was so strong among conservative Protestants in pre-Vatican II America that the mere suggestion of eventual reunion was enough to make people fearful of any ecumenical actions.

The most common argument against merger with the UPC, however, was that mergers in general were unnecessary, because the oneness Jesus prayed for in John 17 was spiritual rather than organic. Albertus Pieters, the irascible former missionary to Japan and professor at Western Seminary, admitted that he could not think of a good reason not to merge. Union was not necessarily a good thing, however. He noted sarcastically that some pro-merger people were infected by the mental disorder "unionitis dogmaticus," which produces hallucinations that disunity is a sin. To hear a

8   Harri Zegerius, "Union With the United Presbyterians—What Next?" *Church Herald*, 13 May 1949, 8. See a critique of Presbyterian liberalism in George Hankamp, letter to the editor, 15 April 1949, 15.

person with this disease talk, he continued, "one would really get the impression that he has a special revelation on the subject. Then he will piously quote John 17:21, 'that they all may be one,' which gives me a pain." Pieters argued that if unity were indeed essential for Christians, Christ would have established it. Since Christ did not, denominations should be understood as human organizations useful for administration, not as signs of sin and brokenness. Pieters insisted that there were simply not enough good reasons to spend the time and energy on merger, when Christianity did not require organic unity among Christians.[9] Both sides claimed to know the will of God. Both appealed to John 17. Each side claimed to have the best answer for the future of the RCA. Those who had come to know some of the UPC people were especially enthusiastic because they experienced the depth of piety and commitment among the UPC people that most of the critics had not encountered.

Merger was approved at General Synod in 1949 but failed to get the necessary votes in the classes. The vote required three-quarters of the classes (thirty-two of forty-two) to approve it by a three-quarters vote. Nineteen classes voted 75 percent, five voted over 50 percent, and eighteen recorded less than 50 percent approval.[10]

There were many good reasons to merge with the UPC, but they did not convince the skeptics. They felt merger was not only unnecessary but also dangerous, because it threatened purity, doctrine, Reformed identity, and the small family feeling in the RCA. It was better to remain safely isolated within the confines of the small denomination. Much of the opposition resulted not from a careful consideration of the wisdom of merger with this particular

9   Albertus Pieters, "Church Union...Why Shouldn't We? Why Should We?" *Church Herald*, 28 January 1949, 12-13.

10 The *Book of Church Order* requires only a majority vote by two-thirds of the classes. UPC polity required approval by three-quarters of the presbyteries. The joint committee recommended the more stringent requirements in its 1949 report. There has been some speculation that Harry Hager, a member of the committee, refused to sign the final report without this clause. He refused to sign it anyway and campaigned quite actively against the merger.

denomination, but from generalized fear and suspicion of other denominations. Opponents of merger tended to overestimate the purity and uniqueness of the RCA and underestimate the quality of commitment in other denominations. They were quick to see differences and magnify them and slow to see the many similarities between the two churches. Ultimately, the fight was not over the character of the UPC and the value of merger, but over who would have the power in the RCA and who would be able to determine the character and future of the denomination.

The Presbyterian Church in the United States

After a decade of quiet on the merger front while the RCA focused on church extension and learning to get along again, in 1961 there were six overtures proposing various mergers. One of these suggested merger with the (southern) Presbyterian Church in the United States (PCUS), three suggested merger with the northern Presbyterian church (called at this time the "United Presbyterian Church, USA," following a merger of the two northern branches), and two suggested entering the talks which would soon be called COCU. Members of the General Synod Executive Committee held conversations with representatives from both the southern PCUS and the northern United Presbyterian Church (UPC) and decided to pursue a relationship with the PCUS, in part because it was less interested in COCU. The choice of the PCUS was also a compromise between eastern churches that preferred to merge with the UPC and those midwestern churches that were not interested in merger at all. The PCUS seemed theologically compatible and geographically complementary. Proponents of merger believed that a larger church with a national scope would have greater influence, a stronger identity, and greater potential for mission and church extension.

As in the merger discussion fifteen years earlier, the Joint Committee of 24 (twelve representatives from each church) made rapid progress. By 1964 the committee concluded that there was substantial agreement between the two churches, and it asked the synod for permission to draft a Plan of Union. The committee was fast, but a number of classes were even faster. The Classes of North and South Grand Rapids overtured in 1964 that if merger occurred, churches should be allowed to opt out with their property and ministers with their pension plans. Before the committee had permission to draft a Plan of Union, the opposition had begun. These early opponents did not debate the merits of merger but threatened that if the RCA approved the merger, they would leave.

In 1964 the General Synod of the Reformed Church received numerous overtures regarding the proposed union, some asking the synod to move ahead, and others asking for an immediate end to the discussion. There was a great deal of heated debate on the floor of the synod. Finally, Donner Atwood, chair of the Overtures Committee, made this speech when he presented his report:

> Fathers and Brethren, the time has come for us to think the unthinkable, to admit the unadmitable, and to speak, in love, the unspeakable; namely, we must openly admit that some of us, on this subject, take positions at opposite poles from each other. If it were only a matter of being divided on church union, serious as that would be we would not be as deeply concerned as we are. But, we must confess to each other and before Almighty God that which is of far graver consequence—we of the Household of Faith, who individually and corporately call Jesus Christ Lord and Saviour, do not trust each other in this matter (as well as in other areas of concern) and therefore are acting and re-acting out of fear of each other, rather than love for each other.[11]

The decision about the plan was postponed for a year to allow for more dissemination of information. The president of the General Synod sent out a pastoral letter encouraging prayer and

---

[11] *Minutes*, 1964, 146.

understanding. In retrospect, the joint committee should have taken this opposition more seriously, because these individuals and classes had a great deal of influence in the Midwest. In 1965, delegates to General Synod voted to move ahead with the Plan of Union.

Opposition continued in the *Church Herald*, however. It appeared that many people made up their minds without reading any of the documents, because strong pronouncements appeared long before the documents did. In a letter written on behalf of the RCA churches in Florida, Raymond Rewerts emphasized the need to preserve the unique and distinctive witness of the RCA. A merger proposal meant that the denomination would "enter into the great ocean of ecumenical unification." The Florida clergy feared that merger meant the loss of the Reformed faith. They called for an end to the discussion, "so that the confession which we consider unique may not be impaired by compromise or by identification with groups whose size so dwarfs us that we would lose all future self-determining ability to protect our Reformed doctrines. We believe that the Holy Spirit is prompting us to this action in the best interests of all concerned in the Church of Jesus Christ."[12] This widespread conviction that the RCA's faith was unique and indeed superior played a significant role in the failure of the merger. Many conservatives were convinced that that RCA had doctrinal standards that precisely interpreted Scripture. Since no other denomination quite had it "right," it made no sense to merge, because a less pure denomination could only dilute the truth present in the RCA. Eastern members, on the other hand, generally recognized that other denominations had both valid doctrinal positions and a common commitment to the gospel.

A similar desire to preserve RCA identity appeared in a letter that accused merger advocates of trying to "give away our denomination and all its institutions without the honest approval of the grass-

---

12 Raymond Rewerts, letter to the editor, *Church Herald*, 29 May 1964, 12.

roots folk who have labored for them, loved them, and paid for them." The midwestern minister then asked, "Are folks who simply desire to keep what God has given them, and what they treasure as a precious heritage, the real cause of division among us?" Like opponents of the UPC merger almost two decades earlier, he predicted that merger with the PCUS would lead the RCA into something even more dangerous—the Blake-Pike proposals (COCU). Here, he said, doctrine would be sacrificed for unity, and this would be apostasy. He believed that Christian unity already existed and did not need to be manufactured.[13]

While some RCA members tried to preserve, protect, and defend RCA identity, the Interchurch Relations Committee tried to promote ecumenical cooperation. At its meeting in 1966, the General Synod passed the policy statement, "The Unity We Seek to Manifest," as mentioned above. It is ironic that the synod could approve phrases such as "ready to cooperate with all Christians" and "prepared to merge with any church when it is clearly the will of God" while there was such strong resistance to an actual merger proposal. Even some of the most conservative Reformed Church members supported ecumenism in theory and could approve a general statement that did not bind them to any particular relationship.

The depth of conviction underlying this document was tested immediately. At its General Assembly meeting two months earlier, the PCUS, somewhat to its own surprise and certainly to the surprise of the RCA, had voted to become a full participant in COCU. Previously both denominations had been observers. The PCUS insisted that it wanted to continue merger negotiations with the RCA, but the action made the RCA very nervous. Whatever

---

13 Rodger Dalman, letter to the editor, *Church Herald*, 21 August 1964, 18. Critics of COCU often referred to it as the Blake-Pike proposals. Eugene Carson Blake had suggested the idea of a multidenominational consultation, and James Pike concurred. Pike was well known for his radical theology, so invoking his name immediately raised questions about the orthodoxy of COCU.

possibility might have remained for approving the PCUS merger was probably destroyed by this action.

The critics actually had very little to say about the PCUS.[14] Until it joined COCU, opposition to merger focused on the loss of RCA identity and vague fears of liberalism. Once COCU was in the picture, however, the gloves were off. RCA members were generally polite in print to the southern Presbyterian gentlemen, but for the nameless, faceless liberals they assumed comprised COCU, there was not even a veneer of civility.

The most vocal and conservative wing of the RCA despised COCU. Despite the preliminary nature of the COCU discussions, some critics were absolutely convinced that this "superchurch" would take over Protestantism and allow bishops and tradition to push aside the Bible. The word "superchurch" had frequently been used to attack the Federal, National, and World Councils of Churches. It evoked images of a large, impersonal bureaucracy that told denominations what to preach, do, and believe. The precious RCA identity would be completely lost in a sea of liberal mediocrity.

A number of classes focused their discontent with merger in overtures concerning polity. Classes repeatedly requested that congregations be allowed to keep their property.[15] Some classes wanted each congregation to vote, which was an interesting shift from Reformed to congregational polity by the same people who were so eager to defend Reformed doctrine and identity. Several

14 I have found no evidence that anyone questioned the segregation practiced by many PCUS congregations or the PCUS belief in the "spirituality of the church," which suggested that the church should not meddle in nonspiritual issues such as racism or politics. Conservative RCA members would likely have agreed with the PCUS on these issues, and perhaps the more liberal members were willing to accept views with which they disagreed for the greater good of a united witness.

15 The Plan of Union did allow for this but required that congregations wait several months after the merger before leaving. Some people thought this was too long and insisted they did not want to become part of the merged church for even a brief time. They also argued that this provision would make them look like schismatics when they withdrew. *Minutes*, 1968, 110.

classes tried to make the merger more difficult by requiring assent from three-quarters of the classes instead of two-thirds, or by requiring each classis to approve it by a two-thirds vote rather than a simple majority. Some classes argued that congregations should be able to instruct their elder delegates or to elect only those who would vote "correctly." Such instruction may have occurred informally, but the synod resisted all other attempts to change the rules at this point.

Despite all the disagreement, in 1968 the General Synod voted 183-103 by secret ballot to approve the merger and send it to the classes for their votes. The classis vote was split roughly in half, with all classes east of Detroit voting for merger, and all classes west of Detroit voting against it. The synod of 1969 that followed is considered one of the most acrimonious ever. Eastern delegates were very frustrated over the defeat of the merger. They hoped that the synod would at least recognize the ecumenical concerns of the eastern churches by joining COCU, but after lengthy debate, the assembly chose to postpone this proposal indefinitely. There was also a heated, late-night debate over membership in the National Council. Withdrawal seems to have been narrowly averted in part by a passionate speech by the general secretary, Marion DeVelder, who said that he would resign his office if the RCA pulled out of the NCC and thereby failed to continue even the most basic ecumenical ties. The lofty promises of ecumenical commitment made in 1966 obviously meant little as the RCA turned down two opportunities to seek unity and narrowly retained a third.

The conflict between the two areas of the RCA was so bitter at this point that Harold Schut, former president of the General Synod and a pastor in Scotia, New York, moved that the denomination consider a plan for the orderly dissolution of the RCA. Many people thought it was impossible for these radically different parts of the church to live together any longer. The disagreements over ecumenism represented deeper conflicts about what it meant to be a church.

A number of factors contributed to the defeat of the PCUS merger. The first was the speed of the process. Although eight years of negotiations seems lengthy, it was a relatively brief process compared to other denominational mergers. The committee moved very quickly from exploration to a merger proposal. It assumed that merger was the right move and probably did not spend enough time promoting it or addressing the reasons for opposition. The joint committee members knew and liked one another, but most clergy and laypeople did not have many opportunities to get to know people from the other denomination, which led to mutual suspicion. Critics in each denomination tended to assume that the other denomination was a monolithic group and failed to recognize the diversity within each church.

A related factor concerns the treatment of dissent and resistance. Some classes objected as early as 1963 and almost every year following. They submitted overtures requesting that congregations have the right to opt out of merger. The synod usually referred these overtures to the joint committee, rather than voting on them directly. Since most synods probably had a majority of delegates who supported merger, it was not difficult to find enough votes to refer the overtures, but this strategy did not take dissent seriously enough, and it further angered the dissenters. The constitutional requirement for a two-thirds vote of the classes meant that the merger needed substantial support beyond a majority. The committee and other merger supporters tended to dismiss critics as right-wing malcontents and probably did not do enough to allay their concerns.

There were a number of questions about the Plan of Union itself. This document was lengthy, somewhat tedious, and focused on denominational machinery. The early enthusiasm that union would yield a greater sense of mission seemed to disappear underneath the bureaucratic language. This made it difficult to find exciting reasons for the merger, and very easy to find reasons to oppose it. Some critics feared that the Plan of Union meant a loss of power and influence for laypeople. They opposed the provision that a presbytery could choose to name a general minister, out of fear that he would function like a bishop. Critics also disliked the loss of the office of deacon (elders would take on deacons' work) because it meant one fewer office for laypeople.

Another serious objection to the Plan of Union resulted from the joint committee's conclusion that it lacked sufficient time to write a new confession of faith along with the Plan of Union, and its decision to assign that task to the new church. Opponents insisted that this was a means to lull people into thinking that their beloved Standards of Unity would be the basis of faith for the new church. Once the new church was formed, it would discard the Standards and write a new confession which would be as liberal as the UPCUSA's Confession of 1967.

Theological Reasons for Hesitance

The high level of suspicion and mistrust evident in some of these objections to merger suggests that there may be more to this debate than a rational discussion of the best way for denominations to do their work. A proposal to merge requires conversation about whether a single denomination will be able to do its work more efficiently and effectively than two. Disagreement over this question is inevitable, since merger results in a sense of loss as well as gain. The nature and intensity of debate in the RCA suggests that the two poles had fundamental disagreements with each other, but rather than address those directly, the church debated ecumenical issues, such as merger or membership in the NCC. It was easier to fight over the relative orthodoxy of another group when the real issue was lack of trust of the others in one's own group. The RCA had an image of itself as a happy family, and happy families are not supposed to fight. But there were significant differences in the two sections of the church that had not been openly and productively addressed.

The first issue was the nature of the church. Reformed churches in the East had a long history of ecumenical cooperation. By the middle of the twentieth century, many of them were in areas in which the once dominant Protestant tradition was rapidly losing ground to Catholics and Jews. The RCA did not have positive name recognition, and the Dutch ethnicity of the church was definitely not a selling point. Many easterners felt that a merger was the only way the RCA could survive. They thought of themselves first as members of the one, holy, catholic church, and secondarily as members of the RCA. Stan Rock, a pastor in Blawenburg, New Jersey, wrote that although he loved the RCA, it could never command his ultimate loyalty, which belonged to the Church of Jesus Christ. Truman Kilborne remarked that it was depressing to read all the arguments for RCA uniqueness, when the RCA was just one regiment in God's army.[16] Easterners appreciated the RCA but valued cooperation over denominational distinctiveness. As Norman Thomas, cochair of the joint committee, wrote, "The Reformed Church is both infinitely more than a mere ethnic convenience and at the same time is infinitely less than the whole body of Christ."[17]

Many of the midwestern churches insisted that denominational distinctiveness was far more important than ecumenical relationships. The RCA was not just one denomination among equals but the nearest approximation to the gospel that could be found in the twentieth century. Harris VerKaik wrote that there were RCA young people who could not sleep out of fear the RCA would not exist when they were adults.[18] Both the distrust of others and the passion for purity seem to be rooted in the formative historical experience of most Midwest churches: the departure of Albertus Van Raalte and others from the Dutch state church in the 1830s and 40s. In an essay in the *Reformed Review*, Jerome DeJong noted that the Midwest resisted merger in part because of their ancestors' experience with the ecclesiastical octopus of the Dutch church. In his mind,

[16] Stan Rock, letter to the editor, *Church Herald*, 20 December 1968, 25; Truman Kilborne, letter to the editor, 21 August 1964, 18.

[17] Norman Thomas, "Looking Toward Union," *Reformed Review* 20/4 (1967): 41.

[18] Harris VerKaik, letter to the editor, *Church Herald*, 11 August 1967, 23.

merger, the Antichrist, and the apostate church were all inextricably linked, and he insisted, "We are not anxious to be caught up in a vast, tyrannical, dictatorial system." He preferred independence to entanglement.[19] It is fascinating that 120 years after Van Raalte departed from the Netherlands, his descendents were still fighting his battles, whether real or imagined. It is a long time to carry a grudge.

The two branches of the RCA also differed over whether the nature of the church was to be a place of refuge and comfort or an always-reforming witness to the world. Eastern churches, in part because of their frequent contact with other religious traditions and with secularism, believed that their role was to be a witness to a changing world, a task that required constant self-evaluation and adjustment. Midwestern congregations preferred that the church be a bulwark against radical change and provide a safe, warm family atmosphere. Merger threatened to make people uncomfortable. In a 1968 overture asking that the General Synod stop talking about merger, the Classis of Chicago argued that "the primary responsibility of the Reformed Church in America, above all other responsibilities" was to preserve "undisruptiveness" within the denominational fellowship. If the merger proposal caused conflict and unrest, then it was best for the church to eliminate such disruption.[20]

A year later after the merger had failed and the Interchurch Relations Committee recommended that the RCA become a full participant in COCU, Gordon Girod castigated denominational executives. "Gentlemen, has it never occurred to you how much more the Reformed Church might accomplish if we had a leadership that led in the direction that our people want to go? You make many excuses for the lack of growth and impact in the Reformed Church: language, old methods, and the like. A much more pressing reason may be found in denominational leaders who are forever seeking to

19 Jerome DeJong, "Ecumenicity and the Reformed Church," *Reformed Review* 20/4 (1967): 18.
20 *Minutes*, 1968, 107.

take our people where they refuse to go."21 For Girod and others, the task of the church was to preserve more than to provoke, to hold fast more than to push forward, to support the status quo more than to take risks.

Eastern clergy were not immune to the appeal of comfort, however. Late in 1968, Norman Vincent Peale explained his views on the merger. He was skeptical at first, he said, because the RCA was such a perfect denomination. Its theology, its people…he wanted to change none of it. But as he studied the PCUS, he said, he realized that these Christians were just like us. Merger was comfortable and therefore acceptable because it did not require dealing with difference.22 Other eastern clergy might not use the word, but clearly they valued the comfort implicit in being part of a larger and better known denomination, and no longer needing to explain the Reformed part of their name.

Norman Thomas found this notion of a comfortable church absolutely appalling. "Any sense of comfort with things as they are is bad Scripture and bad Calvinism and bad theology."23 The church should never be satisfied with its current division or with a comfortable status quo because the church was called to action and initiative. If the church was only led where it wanted to go, it would never go anywhere and it would not really be the church. For Thomas, the task of the church was to provoke more than preserve,

---

21 Gordon Girod, letter to the editor, *Church Herald*, 2 May 1969, 24.
22 Norman Vincent Peale, "Thoughts on the Plan of Union," *Church Herald*, 29 November 1968, 12-13. Peale also said that he opposed membership in COCU and further merger with the northern Presbyterians. The 20 December issue of the *Church Herald* printed three letters from members of the PCUS pointing out that their church was very committed both to COCU and to eventual merger with the northern Presbyterians. The PCUS was divided over this issue of further merger. Some PCUS members agreed with these letters, but some of the more conservative southern Presbyterians hoped that merger with the RCA would mean they did not have to merge with the liberal northern group.
23 Thomas, "Looking Toward Union," 41.

to push forward more than to hold fast, and to take risks more than to support the status quo.

The second theological issue concerns the nature of the faith, or the beliefs that formed the core of denominational identity. Some people spoke of the faith as the whole living, growing, dynamic Christian tradition. It was the story of God's relationship with humanity and human participation in the larger story. This faith changed and grew over time, but it was always centered in God, which meant that it was steady and utterly reliable.

Other RCA members, usually the more conservative, frequently spoke of "the faith once delivered to the saints." Faith in this sense meant the human response to God, or that which Christians were required to believe, think, and know. The correct faith had been delivered first to the authors of the Bible, and then to the authors of the sixteenth-and seventeenth-century Reformed confessions. Contemporary Christians were to articulate their faith exactly as did the Reformed confessions. A layperson wrote to the *Church Herald*, "If every member of our Church would refresh his mind on the basic doctrines explained in the Heidelberg Catechism and the Canons of Dort and would hold to these as the true understanding of Scripture, I would have no fear for our church."[24] Faith for this author was not the shared story of the Christian tradition, but the Reformed interpretation of it. He implied that those Christians who affirm the Augsburg or Westminster Confessions do not have the true understanding of Scripture.

If the faith is primarily defined as human response and belief, then it is possible to have it wrong, or allow the faith to slip away. The faith needed to be protected from anything that would destroy or weaken it, such as compromise, ecumenism, and liberalism. Several writers insisted that a merger would lead to the loss of all the forefathers fought for and held dear.

Those who saw the faith as a set of documents and beliefs believed that ecumenical relationships should only exist with those

[24] Wesley Harmsen, letter to the editor, *Church Herald*, 13 January 1969, 17.

churches with which there was substantial doctrinal agreement. Those who viewed the faith as God's story and God's action were more willing to cooperate based on a shared commitment to a common faith. Churches did not need to agree on every aspect of doctrine in order to work together.

A third theological issue concerned the roles that trust and fear played in the worldview of RCA members. "The Unity We Seek to Manifest" statement approved in 1966 contained the phrase, "trusting in the Holy Spirit for guidance." Overall, trust was in short supply. Donner Atwood, a pastor who had organized a group of pro-merger people, received a number of angry letters. In most of them, he wrote to friends, "Our very Christian motivation and Christian commitment to Jesus Christ as Lord and Saviour has been called into question because we favor the Union, which they opposed."[25] Herman Ridder, president of Western Theological Seminary, commented after the failed merger vote that proponents of merger had erred in assuming that people needed more information, "when what they really needed was not facts but the ability to trust."[26]

The Midwest saw the eastern churches as liberal zealots for ecumenism, whose declining membership demonstrated their lack of commitment and spiritual vitality. Midwestern people did not trust the eastern bureaucrats who ran the church, and they did not trust the PCUS or COCU. A few particularly vocal and angry clergy and laypeople wrote often in the *Church Herald* and formed committees and newsletters designed to fight the merger proposal. Their accusations and innuendoes further undermined trust. Eastern RCA members were also very frustrated with the midwestern churches, which were perceived as separatist reactionaries who squelched new ideas in order to preserve their purity.

---

25 Donner Atwood to Norman and Ruth Peale, Dec. 30, 1968. Thomas papers, RCA Archives.
26 Herman Ridder, "A Time to Heal," *Reformed Review* 23/2 (1970): 73.

Opponents of ecumenism believed that they were protecting the church and the true Reformed faith from those who would damage or destroy it. Like Elijah, they claimed to be very zealous for the Lord (1 Kings 19:10,14), but it might be asked if zeal for God ever masks a lack of trust in God's ability to protect God's church. Some of their rhetoric and actions implied that they had to take on God's role, as it were, and expend astonishing amounts of energy to protect the church from the PCUS and COCU. Some of that energy might have been directed to enemies more worthy of their attention.

The pro-merger people, mostly easterners, demonstrated their own lack of trust in God's ability to preserve the church. A common argument for merger claimed that the RCA could not survive without becoming Presbyterian. Others argued that the only effective way to witness to the city was ecumenical cooperation. Howard Hageman asked, "If we neglect this opportunity [to merge]...what will become of us and what account of ourselves shall we give to [God]?" Norman Thomas asked, "How can the church witness to its Lord when by its fragmented witness it is disobedient to its Lord?"[27] One response to these questions is that, merger or no merger, the church will continue to bear witness to the gospel the way it has for centuries, by the grace of God. The efficacy of the gospel does not depend on the unity of the church or any other human endeavor or accomplishment.

Three Decades Later

In concord there may be strength, but debates about concord nearly divided the Reformed Church in half. Merger proposals did not create discord within the RCA, but they certainly exacerbated internal suspicion and mistrust. The denomination spent an enormous amount of time, energy, and money pursuing, debating, and opposing these two mergers. The end result of both efforts was the painful realization that many RCA members did not like or trust

[27] Howard Hageman, "To Unite or Not to Unite," *Church Herald*, 24 January 1969, 22; Thomas, "Looking Toward Union," 41.

each other. A denomination cannot reach concord with another denomination when its own divisions are so severe.

In retrospect, it appears that both the fears and the hopes about merger were overstated and unrealistic. Merger probably would not have been either a panacea or an abject failure. Proponents of merger hoped that a united church would have a stronger witness to the world. Norman Thomas argued that people did not pay attention to the church because of its disunity, and he believed that merger could be a healing gesture which would be a step toward the salvation of humankind.[28] Proponents of the Lutheran-Reformed Formula of Agreement made a similar claim almost thirty years later. Both arguments presume that the church has a significant impact on the world and that the world cares what happens to the church. It has become quite clear over the past three decades that mainline Protestantism has relatively little voice in contemporary society, and no amount of restructuring or merging is likely to change that fact.

This analysis of ecumenical hesitance suggests that the RCA needs to discern some productive ways to work through its differences. The RCA displayed a similar tendency to hesitance and second thoughts after approving the Formula of Agreement in 1997. Bitter debate followed, not about the Lutherans but about the United Church of Christ and its beliefs about homosexuality. Discussion about homosexuality within the RCA up to that point had been so painful and difficult that the General Synod declared a moratorium for several years. But if RCA members could not fight with each other directly, they could and did fight about the United Church of Christ. In the end, the debate marred the relationship between the RCA and the UCC but left the RCA no closer to resolving its own differences about homosexuality.

During the last thirty years, the Reformed Church in America has experienced significant changes. The eastern churches have lost

28 Norman Thomas, "Why I Favor Union with the Presbyterians in the U.S." *Church Herald*, 27 December 1968, 12-14.

members and influence while the midwestern churches have gained members and influence. The Far West now offers a new geographical, theological, and ecclesiastical dimension to the RCA. The old categories of liberal and conservative are undergoing revision as patterns of worship and polity change. Denominational concord is as elusive as ever. Each geographical section of the church has been shaped in particular ways by its distinctive experience. The varied theological perspectives represented in the RCA arise out of genuine commitment to the gospel. The future of the RCA will depend, I believe, on whether the diverse groups and positions within it can find concord, not in complete agreement, but in mutual respect and appreciation.

3

The Theological Roots of the RCA's Ecumenical Disposition

Paul R. Fries

From its reformational beginnings, the Reformed tradition has produced figures passionate for Christian unity. Calvin attempted to bring into fellowship the churches of the Swiss cantons, and his desire for *communio* with the Lutherans was so intense that McNeill and Nichols described it as an "almost pathetic craving."[1] Theodore Beza, Calvin's "apostle Paul," shared his teacher's desire for *communio* with the Lutherans, hoping the *Harmonia confessionum fidei*, prepared under his guidance, would bridge the gap between the two traditions.[2] As is well known, the much praised Heidelberg Catechism was intended to bring together opposing groups, although precisely which groups is still a matter of scholarly debate, as Lyle D. Bierma has shown in a recent monograph examining the sacramental theology of the catechism.[3] Although the Prussian Union of 1817

---

1 John T. McNeill and James Hasting Nichols, *Ecumenical Testimony* (Philadelphia: Westminster Press, 1974), 23.
2 Ibid., 36-37.
3 Lyle D. Bierma, *The Doctrine of the Sacraments in the Heidelberg Catechism: Melanchtonian, Calvinist, or Zwinglian?* (Princeton: Princeton Theological Seminary, 1999), 7-8. Bierma draws these conclusions concerning the purpose of the catechism in regard to the sacraments: "The doctrine of the sacraments in the Heidelberg Catechism—is it then Melanchthonian, Calvinist,

35

has been called a "shotgun wedding," significant Reformed voices, including that of Schleiermacher, supported it, while in the United States the *Kirchenverein* of 1841, which would later unite with the German Reformed Church, was accomplished, in part, through Reformed leadership. When the canvas of twentieth-century ecumenical interaction is surveyed, an impressive panorama of Reformed participation is displayed. A "who's who" of leadership in the ecumenical movement of the past century leading to the formation of the World Council of Churches and the establishment of national councils around the world would be heavily weighted with the names of prominent Reformed leaders and theologians. The same could be said of the scores of national and international bilateral consultations occurring throughout the world.

At the same time, an ecumenical reserve, even resistance, can be identified within the churches of the Reformed tradition. Post-Reformation Reformed theology employed a neoscholastic theology to fortify the boundaries of orthodoxy and developed "exclusionist" interpretations of the marks of the true church. The eighteenth and nineteenth centuries witnessed myriad divisions within the churches of the tradition in the name of orthodoxy, but also fractures prompted by nationalism, social values, and spiritual practice. One need only to view branching charts of Reformed churches in the Netherlands and Presbyterian churches in the United States for vivid and depressing ideograms of Reformed divisiveness. And if Reformed denominations and leaders stood at the vanguard of the ecumenical movement of the twentieth century, some of the most formidable opposition to these developments was mounted contemporaneously by churches and individuals who marched under the flag of Reformed doctrine.

or (late-) Zwinglian? In the last analysis, it is none of these and it is all three. Situated in the middle of the spectrum of Protestant opinion, the Heidelberg Catechism's position on the sacraments was broad enough to encompass the whole range of views that lay between Zwingli on the left and the strict Lutherans on the right," 42.

Where has the Reformed Church in America (RCA) found itself in the swirling currents and counter currents of modern ecumenism?[4] Friend or foe? A case could be made for both positions. The church has voted down several plans for church union and declined membership in the Consultation on Church Union. Yet the denomination was a charter member of the World Council of Churches, the National Council of Churches, and the World Alliance of Reformed Churches. Recently the RCA entered, kicking and screaming, into the Formula of Agreement, but for all the sound and fury the denomination did in fact sign on, and with a decisive vote.

I believe that the Reformed Church is, in fact, ecumenically disposed, and in making this judgment, I am not referring only to those events in the life of the church which have been heralded as ecumenical achievements. There is a less visible and differently contoured ecumenism in the RCA that has often been overlooked or disregarded by church leaders. Staunch opponents of denominational ecumenism have in many instances deeply engaged fellowship with Christians of other traditions at the grassroot level. I will refer, in this essay, to such grassroots ecumenism as "heart to heart" fellowship,[5] to distinguish it from the more familiar "church to church" fellowship among traditions. My purpose here is not to provide a survey of these types of ecumenism in the church, but rather to identify the roots of each in the theology of the Reformed tradition. I will demonstrate that Calvin's ecclesiology and sacramentology, given expression in the Belgic Confession and Heidelberg Catechism, provide the theological foundation of the RCA's commitment to church-to-church fellowship. I will then provide evidence that the denomination's heart-to-heart ecumenism also has its roots in the confessional theology of the church. By

---

4   The term "ecumenical" is used broadly in this essay, as it is in contemporary usage, to denote any type of activity that draws churches and traditions together. It does not suggest any definition of the unity, e.g., full communion.
5   I am using the word "fellowship" as a substitute for the technical *communio*.

establishing the Reformed pedigree of each, I will be positioned to argue—even plead—that these two modes of ecumenism be seen no longer as mutually exclusive, but rather as complementary and equally necessary.

Church-to-Church Ecumenism

First, church-to-church ecumenism. Evidence that Calvin's ecclesiology plays a major role in this type of ecumenical disposition in the Reformed tradition need not be drawn from passages in which he explicitly speaks of unity, but may rather be distilled from his broader writing on the church. In the *Institutes of the Christian Religion* Calvin writes,

> …that we may clearly grasp the sum of this matter, we must proceed by the following steps: the church universal is a multitude gathered from all nations; it is divided and dispersed in separate places, but agrees on the one truth of divine doctrine, and is bound by the bond of the same religion. Under it are thus included individual churches, disposed in towns and villages according to human need, so that each rightly has the name and authority of the church.[6]

The universal church is understood to be constituted by the truth of God's teaching and the bond of religion, that is, Word and Spirit. It is prior to the local church that is derivative from it. Notice that Calvin is not speaking of the universal church as a single historical entity but rather in terms of a fellowship, a *communio*, effected by Christ.

As the universal church is prior to the congregation, so is the congregation prior to the individual. Philip Butin, in an admirable

---

[6] John Calvin, *Institutes of the Christian Religion*, ed. John T. McNeill, trans. Ford Lewis Battles (Philadelphia: Westminster Press, 1960), IV.1.9. I have used Donald K. McKim's abridgment of Battles's translation here and below. *Calvin's Institutes: Abridged Edition*, ed. Donald K. McKim (Louisville: Westminster John Knox Press, 2001).

monograph on Calvin's ecclesiology, uses the phrase "contextualized grace"[7] to describe the reformer's understanding of the church. Through this contextualization of grace, the gospel is offered to the world, the elect are incorporated into the community of faith, and believers are nurtured and regenerated. Although the *Institutes* presents soteriology (Book III) before ecclesiology (Book IV), this should not be interpreted to mean that in Calvin's view the church is an affiliation of those who have received grace. Christ died for the church and thus for the individuals incorporated into the church— not the reverse.[8]

It cannot be stated too emphatically that Calvin has the visible church in mind when he speaks in this manner of the church. A common misunderstanding holds that when Calvin writes of the universality of the church and the call and regeneration of the believer, he is referring only to the invisible church of the truly elect. This is not the case; there is no salvation apart from the visible church. The means of grace do not appear in the invisible church: here there is no preaching of the gospel, no administration of the sacraments. It is the actual, observable, historic church that contextualizes grace. It is indeed the case that grace is communicated through it only to the elect members of the invisible church, but that does not mean that some sort of division of the house is permissible. This God will accomplish, but not until the final judgment. Until that time, all those in the visible church are to be regarded as also being the elect members of the invisible church.

Here we find the foundation of Calvin's teaching on the certainty of election. We are counseled not to probe the mysteries of God's eternal plan, nor are we to attempt to assess the health of our faith.[9]

---

7   Philip Butin, *Reformed Ecclesiology: Trinitarian Grace According to Calvin* (Princeton: Princeton Theological Seminary, 1994), 13.

8   Butin, *Reformed Ecclesiology*, 16 n. 45.

9   Calvin does acknowledge that good works complement and testify to election but insists that assurance cannot be based on anything but the promise of the Word. See Calvin, III.14.18-20.

We look to the proclamation of the Word of God, the promise of Christ, for our assurance.

> For just as those engulf themselves in a deadly abyss who, to make their election more certain, investigate God's eternal plan apart from his Word, so those who rightly and duly examine it as to what is contained in his Word reap the inestimable fruit of comfort.[10]

The Word that is the ground and assurance of the elect's call is the Word proclaimed in the church—a visible Word in a visible church. That the church is the arena of saving grace—the only arena for Calvin—is given additional testimony in his discussion of the power of the keys. Referring to divine forgiveness, he writes:

> This benefit so belongs to the church that we cannot enjoy it unless we abide in communion with the church.…It is dispensed to us through the ministers and pastors of the church, either by the preaching of the gospel or by the administration of the sacraments; and herein chiefly stands out the power of the keys, which the Lord has conferred upon the society of believers.[11]

Assurance of salvation thus depends on participation in the church, the body of Christ where the gospel is preached and sacraments administered.

One of the standards of the RCA, the Belgic Confession, contributes to our understanding at this point. This statement, written by Guido de Brès in 1561, follows closely the French Confession authored by Calvin, and was sent to him for approval. A number of the reformer's revisions were incorporated into it.[12] It is not Article 27, which presents the doctrine of the church, that

---

10   Calvin, *Institutes*, III.24.4
11   Calvin, *Institutes*, IV.1.22.
12   Jan Rohls, *Reformed Confessions: Theology from Zurich to Barmen* (Louisville: Westminster John Knox Press, 1997), 17.

interests me at this point but rather Article 33, concerning the sacraments. The confession describes them, in Augustinian language, as "visible signs and seals of something internal and invisible, by means of which God works in us through the power of the Holy Spirit. So they are not empty and hollow signs to fool and deceive us, for their truth is Jesus Christ without whom they would be nothing," words that reflect Calvin's lengthier discussion in the *Institutes*.[13] While not efficacious through their own working, they are both signs and instruments of the Spirit's activity. As our bodies are nourished by food, de Brès reasons, so is our soul nourished by the body and blood of Jesus, which is Spiritually mediated to us.[14] In the sacramental action of eating, then, there is a kind of a parable or analogy, which testifies to, and as "visible words" helps effect, the communication of grace.

By pointing to these teachings of the Belgic Confession, I am suggesting that there is a parallel structure of visible/invisible running through both Calvin's ecclesiology and sacramentology. In each case, the invisible is not caused by the visible, but neither is invisible grace possible apart from the visible means. Thus at the heart of the ecclesiology, and consequently soteriology, is the doctrine of visibility. The invisible can only exist in and through the visible. Such applies not only to Word and sacrament, but also to the unity of the church. To the degree that a Reformed theological culture draws from Calvin and the confessions of the sixteenth century, it will be ecumenically disposed. Thus the theological source of Calvin's "almost pathetic craving" for visible unity with the Lutherans: invisible unity for him would be no unity at all. For Calvin, the disunity of evangelical churches was a rebuff of the Holy Spirit.[15]

---

13 Calvin, *Institutes*, IV.14.1-3.
14 The word "Spiritually" is capitalized here in that it refers to the working of the Holy Spirit.
15 The term "unity" is used here to mean *communio* and is not intended to suggest what in our time is called organic union.

It is true that Calvin's writings are spiked with harsh polemic against the Anabaptists, as is the Belgic Confession, and that the reformer was in constant battle with Roman Catholics and others. His minimalist definition of the true church, shared with the Lutherans, *viz.*, where the Word is truly preached and the sacraments properly administrated, precluded both Catholics and Anabaptists because Calvin did not believe either met the evangelical standard. When, as was the case in the twentieth century, the true preaching of the Word and proper administration of the sacraments were understood more inclusively, Calvin's uncompromising affirmation of visibility created a powerful impetus for the achievement of a visible unity which potentially excluded no Christian body. The theological roots of Reformed ecumenical vigor in the past century, and the inclination to church-to-church ecumenism in the RCA, are to be found in the theology of Calvin and the confessions of the church.

Heart-to-Heart Ecumenism

There are members of the RCA who, while being skeptical about the World Council of Churches and suspicious of the National Council of Churches, will nonetheless gladly engage in the second form of ecumenism I am discussing here—heart-to-heart ecumenism. For such Christians, formal agreements between denominations are far less important than the fellowship rising out of spiritual experience. Hearts warmed by Christ find unity regardless of church affiliation and allow believers from various backgrounds to ignore the issues that historically divided them. Often Reformed champions of church-to-church ecumenism wrongly, in my opinion, dismiss such *communio* as expressions of a pietism alien to the teachings of the reformation. To the contrary, the deepest sources of this second type of ecumenism are to be located in the tradition itself, especially in the confessional standard, the Canons of the Synod of Dort (1618-1619).

The events at Dordrecht have special importance for the Reformed Church in America. Less than a decade after the synod adjourned, the first church of our denomination was established on Manhattan Island, and when, after the American Revolution, what is now the RCA gained independence from the Classis of Amsterdam, the order, standards, and liturgies of the new church were based on the Canons of Dort, applied through the Explanatory Articles of 1792.[16]

As was the case with the Council of Nicaea, the Synod of Dort was called and financed by the civil government. It was an international council with representatives from the Palatinate, Nassau, Hesse, East Friesland, Bremen, England, Scotland, and Switzerland.[17] The presenting issue, the teachings of the followers of Arminius on predestination in opposition to those held by the followers of Theodore Beza, is well known and does not need to be rehearsed here. What is not as well understood is that the canons deal with far more than the doctrine of election; they, in fact, present rich teaching on the Holy Spirit, the church, and regeneration.[18]

In attempting to redeem election from the charge of determinism on the one hand and quietism on the other, the writers of the Canons of Dort meticulously detailed their understanding of the manner in which the Holy Spirit engages the human spirit in the regeneration of the elect. A kind of psychology of appropriation results, in which the true and full participation of men and women in the saving action of the Spirit is underscored. As the canons state:

> When God carries out (God's) good pleasure in the elect,
> or works true conversion in them, God not only sees to it

---

16 The text of the Explanatory Articles is available in Daniel J. Meeter, *Meeting Each Other: In Doctrine, Liturgy, and Government*, Historical Series of the Reformed Church in America, no. 24 (Grand Rapids: Eerdmans, 1993), 61-144.

17 Rohls, *Reformed Confessions*, 22.

18 Respectively, pneumatology, ecclesiology, and soteriology.

that the gospel is proclaimed to them outwardly, and enlightens their minds powerfully by the Holy Spirit so that they may rightly understand and discern the things of the Spirit of God, but, by the effective operation of the same regenerating Spirit, God also penetrates into the inmost being of people, opens the closed heart, softens the hard heart, and circumcises the heart that is uncircumcised. God infuses new qualities into the will, making the dead will alive, the evil one good, the unwilling one willing, and the stubborn one compliant.... *As a result, all those in whose hearts God works in this marvelous way are certainly, unfailingly, and effectively reborn and do actually believe. And then the will, now renewed, is not only activated and motivated by God, but in being activated by God is also itself active. For this reason, human beings themselves, by that grace they have received, are also rightly said to believe and repent.*[19]

The examination of the inner dynamics of salvation extends in the canons beyond regeneration to the assurance of election. When Calvin addressed the question, "Am I truly elect?" he answered by pointing to the Word of God. Good works may provide confirmation, but confidence may not be based on them. Dort, however, veers at this point from the father of Reformed faith, exhibiting no such reserve about discerning signs of election. Following the teaching of the Heidelberg Catechism (Question 86) and of Theodore Beza, the canons hold that evidence of election may be identified. But Dort differs from these in that signs of election are located only not in *outward* but also, and perhaps more importantly, in *inward* signs—not only in good works, but also in what we would today call religious experience. Permit me to quote again from the canons:

---

[19] *The Canons of Dort: A New Translation for the Reformed Church in America* (Reformed Church Press, 1991), III-IV.11-12. Italics added.

Assurance of their eternal and unchangeable election to salvation is given to those in due time, though by various stages and in differing measure. Such assurance comes not by inquisitive searching into the hidden and deep things of God, *but by noticing within themselves, with spiritual joy and holy delight, the unmistakable fruits of election pointed out in God's Word—fruits such as true faith in Christ, a childlike fear of God, a godly sorrow for their sins, a hunger and thirst for righteousness, and so on.*[20]

In the vocabulary of Reformed scholasticism, this doctrine is referred to as the *syllogismus mysticus*. Suggested here is this syllogism: Scripture promises certain spiritual experiences to the elect; I recognize these experiences in my own life, and therefore I can be assured of my election. In these teachings of the canons regarding the internal signs of election, we have what may be regarded as the theological charter of Dutch Reformed pietism. It is true that William Ames and other Puritans influenced the development of experiential Reformed Christianity, but they did not provide its theological bedrock. It is rather the theology of Dort that provided confessional foundation for the so-called *Nadere Reformatie*, and, in the nineteenth century, the *Réveil*, the latter playing a role in the *Afscheiding* of 1834 that eventually brought immigrants from the Netherlands to the American Midwest, forming congregations, some uniting with the Reformed Church in the East.

In such pietism, unity by baptism or confession is eclipsed by a fellowship of the heart. While the believer searched for *internal* signs, such signs could and did receive public testimony and thus became the basis for a special fellowship within the congregation. This permitted religious experience to become in some churches an indication of the truly converted, in contrast to mere church members. When the experience of Christ came to be disassociated from a narrow Calvinistic orthodoxy for many Reformed Christians,

[20] *Canons*, I.12 Italics added.

the basis for heart-to-heart ecumenism was theologically established. Now another implicit syllogism was at work: the experience of Christ is the mark of the true believer; you testify convincingly to such experience, and therefore I accept you as a brother or sister in Christ. "Born-again" Methodists, Baptists, Lutherans, and even Roman Catholics could come into *communio* with Reformed Christians, bypassing the often-tortured efforts of denominational leaders and theologians to bring their churches into church-to-church fellowship.

Ecumenism in the Spirit's Embrace

In demonstrating that both church-to-church and heart-to-heart ecumenism flow from the headwaters of the confessional Dutch Reformed tradition, I wish to affirm the importance of both and, further, appeal for an understanding of ecumenism that excludes neither. A truly ecumenical church must embrace and exhibit both types; they must be regarded as not competitive but complementary. An ecumenical perspective drawing on the rich Reformed teachings concerning the Holy Spirit will bring the institutional and personal together in an indivisible unity.

Reformed ecclesiology is predicated on Christ's Ascension and the gift of the Spirit. Perhaps to a greater degree than any other, the Reformed tradition has located the full activity of Christ after the Ascension in the Holy Spirit. When Reformed theology speaks of Christ in the church or world, such statements always carry an implied explanatory note: through the activity of the Holy Spirit. This point is forcibly made in the somewhat technical language of *A Common Calling*, the study that provided the theological basis for *The Formula of Agreement*:

> Reformed theologians taught the local circumscription of Christ's body in heaven. For them, this assertion seemed to be the clear implication of the ascension and was necessary to free the Supper from wrong sacramental magic to its

true, intended spiritual use. This did not mean the denial of Christ's lordship over all the world here and now or the underestimation of his divinity. What was feared was that the philosophical construction of a ubiquity of Christ's human nature would jeopardize the reality of the historical incarnation and make the soteriological work of the Spirit redundant.[21]

The bodily Christ no longer is to be found on earth, even in the bread and wine of the eucharist—it is "circumscribed" in heaven. Christ is present to us in the eucharist, in the church, only by the activity of the Spirit who links us to the ascended Lord.

In a remarkable series of questions and answers, the Heidelberg Catechism makes this linkage clear. The catechism teaches that eyewitnesses testify to the removal of Christ from the world (Q. 46), and, consequently, that in his human nature Christ is not on earth, although in his divinity, and through his Spirit, he is never absent from us (Q. 47). The catechism then inquires, Does this mean that the human and divine natures are divided? Stating concisely what has been called the *extra Calvinisticum*, the answer refuses this possibility, explaining, in effect, that the divinity of the second person is omnipresent, but also fully present in union with the human nature of Christ (Q. 48). Christ's ascension produces a set of *beneficia Christi* (benefits or gifts of Christ):

> First, he is our advocate in heaven in the presence of his Father. Second, we have our flesh as a full guarantee in heaven that Christ our head, will also take us, his members up to himself. Third, he sends us, as a guarantee on earth, his Spirit by whose power we seek what is above, where Christ is sitting at the right hand of God, and not things that are on earth. (Q. 49)

---

21 *A Common Calling*, ed. Keith F.Nickle and Timothy F. Lull (Minneapolis: Augsburg Fortress, 1993), 47.

This catechism's narration concludes with testimony to the benefits of what the older theology called the session of Christ, that is, by the Ascension (*not* the Incarnation). Christ is head of the church, and lavishes gifts on its members (Qs. 50-51).

The ascended Christ is therefore the substance not only of the sacraments (as we saw when we examined the Belgic Confession), but of the church itself. Through the Spirit, Christ takes shape in the life of the community of faith. The preamble to the *Book of Church Order of the Reformed Church in America*, in its reference to ministry, provides another example of the ways the Christological head of the church forms the pneumatological (Spiritual) body:

> The principle of the equality of the ministry, conceived now in its broadest sense as including the functions of the elder and deacon, is based upon the fact that the entire ministerial or pastoral office is summed up in Jesus Christ himself in such a way that he is, in a sense, the only one holding that office. Every ministerial function is found preeminently in him. By his Holy Spirit he distributes these functions among those whom he calls to serve in his name.[22]

Christ is the only true bishop of the church, ministering in and through the offices and the baptized people of God. And this ministry, the offices, baptism, and the people of God itself are works of the Holy Spirit.

The understanding of the church and its ministry reflected in the standards and polity of the Reformed Church in America precludes speaking of the church as an incarnational reality, as is popular today. There is one and only one Incarnation, the Word becoming flesh in Jesus Christ, and this enfleshment of the Word was not undone either by the Resurrection or the Ascension, but continues in heaven, as has been indicated in the above discussion of the Heidelberg Catechism. Classical Reformed theology distinguished

---

[22] *Book of Church Order* (New York: Reformed Church Press, 2001), 1.

between the messianic *incarnatio* (incarnation) and pneumatological *inhabitio* (inhabitation or indwelling)—both representing "God with us," but in different ways. The church is thus not an extension of the incarnation, nor does it depend on the ubiquitous body of Christ. It is a work of the Holy Spirit.

This work involves not only persons, but "things" as well. We have seen that in baptism and the Lord's Supper, God the Spirit uses "things" such as water, bread, and wine to communicate grace. And God the Spirit also uses "things" such as office, ordination, and installation to realize the ministry of Christ in and through the church, as stated in the *Book of Church Order*. These things become not only instruments of the Spirit of Christ, but also signs of the Lord's presence in the world. A denomination may also be described as a "thing" that represents Christ in the world and through which he is served. When denominations stand apart from one another, unable to enter fellowship, a "counter-sign" is formed. Rather than reconciliation in Christ, divided churches signify the sinful fragmentation everywhere evident in a fallen world. Both the work of Christ, and witness to him, are seriously jeopardized by the disunity of the church, and the Spirit is surely grieved.

Clearly "things" such as the sacraments, office, structure, as important as they are, cannot be divorced from the persons to whom they relate. A formal declaration of communion bringing together denominations has little meaning if congregations and individual Christians remain suspicious of one another. The Spirit of Christ, as has been discussed above, draws the faithful together and binds them on the basis of their experience of the love of Christ. Yet individual believers are parts of congregations governed by consistories who receive grace through the preaching of the Word and the administration of the sacraments—through the indispensable "things" of the church. Church-to-church ecumenism runs the danger of empty form; heart-to-heart ecumenism tends toward the superficial and ephemeral. The two types belong together as do body and soul.

We are now able to draw this discussion to a close, having seen that both church-to-church and heart-to-heart ecumenism exist in the Spirit's embrace. In our examination of Reformed ecclesiology, we established that for Calvin and the RCA standards, unity is not something that may or may not be made visible. Visibility *constitutes* unity, and any talk of an invisible unity is as nonsensical as to speak of an invisible church apart from the visible church. Thus denominations in fellowship ought not be regarded as a sign of unity, but its reality. In our examination of Reformed soteriology, we saw that the experience of Christ and his gifts as a sign of election prepared the soil for experiential Reformed Christianity and allowed Reformed believers to enter fellowship with others Christians on the basis of mutually recognized experience. By Calvin's principle of visibility, the fellowship of believers also ought not be regarded as a sign of unity, but its reality. And yet neither is a *full* manifestation of oneness is Christ; together they present, if not a complete, a richer and *fuller* expression of Christian unity.

The Reformed Church in America, it seems to me, has been given a rich theological heritage—one which has produced much sustenance for the church and nation. By exploring the theological roots of the faith and practice we now engage, we both enter fellowship with our forbears and find coordinates for a faithful future. We may discover that elements within the church which have stood in opposition can be made to cooperate and this for the well-being of the church catholic and in the service of Christ. Church-to-church and heart-to-heart ecumenism, both with their confessional pedigrees, offer prime examples of this possibility.

4

Ecumenism in Reformed Perspective

Karel Blei

In Reformed perspective, what is "ecumenism"? Let me take as a starter the definition given by the document called *An Ecumenical Mandate for the Reformed Church in America*: "Ecumenism can be defined as that movement within the church which seeks to give visible expression to the unity that all believers have in Jesus Christ."[1] Several elements in this definition strike me in particular. I would like to make a few comments.

First, ecumenism is called a "movement within the church." What church is meant here? The Reformed Church in America? I rather suppose that what is meant is what we might call the church of the Creed, that is, the "Holy Catholic Church" in which we affirm our belief when we say the Apostles' Creed. It is that church which, according to the Reformed tradition, could be described as "the

---

1 *An Ecumenical Mandate for the Reformed Church in America* (Grand Rapids: RCA Distribution Center, n.d.), 5. The General Synod approved this document (first published in *Minutes of the General Synod, RCA,* 1995, 174-86) "for use in the Reformed Church in America as a foundation and guide for its ecumenical relations" in 1996. *Minutes of the General Synod, RCA* (hereafter, *Minutes*), 1996, 197.

unity of all believers," the phrase we find mentioned here in connection with the goal of ecumenism ("giving" to that unity "visible expression"). As the Belgic Confession says (Art. 27), the church is "a holy congregation and assembly of true Christian believers." It is true that there is a slight difference in wording. "Congregation" is not exactly the same as "unity." Generally, we prefer to speak of the church as the "congregation," the "communion," of the believers. That, to our understanding, leaves more space for diversity among the believers. But a unity need not be a uniformity. Of "communion," the word "union" is an integral part. A congregation that is not a unity, that even does not want to be a unity, is not a congregation either! In the word "congregation," we have to take the prefix "con" (meaning "together") seriously. The question then is, however: is "ecumenism" really the movement within that church (Christ's church) to make *itself* visible? If so, then, by implication, that church in itself is said to be *not* visible. I will come back to that point in a moment. My question now is: how about ecumenism then? Is that a *visible* movement? Yes, of course; how could it be otherwise? But is it therefore a visible movement within an invisible church? Is that feasible at all?

My second comment is connected to my first; it also has to do with the use of the word "church." How is the church of the Creed, the church we believe, related to the church we see (say, the Reformed Church of America, or the Netherlands Reformed Church)? What does it mean that in both cases the same word, "church," is being used? In the above definition of ecumenism, remarkably enough, that question is not addressed. One might think any definition of ecumenism incomplete if it does not take up that crucial issue.

My third comment addresses another missing element in the above definition of ecumenism. Not mentioned is the idea that ecumenism has to do with the community, or even unity, of the churches, the denominations, plural. It seems as if the only thing that matters in ecumenism is the unity of "all believers." But is not ecumenism, as it started in the beginning of the twentieth century, the movement that aims at overcoming the shame of the fact that *churches* are divided and even opposed to each other? Does it not aim at *inter alia*, overcoming the divisions between church denominations and between church traditions as such? An echo of this aim is still to be found in article III of the Constitution of the World Council of Churches, which was originally constituted as the embodiment of the ecumenical movement.[2] I quote the new text of this article, as adopted by the Harare Assembly in 1998: "the primary purpose of the fellowship of churches in the World Council of Churches is to call one another to visible unity in one faith and in one eucharistic fellowship, expressed in worship and common life in Christ, through witness and service to the world." Here, it is not just the believers but the churches themselves who are supposed to call each other, and to be called by each other, to unity. More precisely, they are said to call each other "to *advance* towards that unity."[3] In other words, concrete steps will have to be taken to cross the boundaries that still keep the denominations separated. Now, I do not state that the RCA *Ecumenical Mandate* entirely loses sight of this element of ecumenism. Its section II deals with "expressions of ecumenism" like "cooperative ecumenism," "conciliar ecumenism," and "dialogical ecumenism," in which church-to-church relations are indeed at stake[4]; and section III, on the subject of "establishing and maintaining ecumenical relations," mentions "other

---

2 It is true that the Harare Assembly in 1998 adopted an amendment, according to which the World Council is instead said to "*serve* the one ecumenical movement" (italics added). The amendment was an attempt to take into account that the ecumenical movement itself is broader than its embodiment in the council (a fact that, to be sure, the World Council had never denied). Both the original text of article III and the amended text adopted in Harare are included in the *Assembly Workbook Harare 1998* (Geneva: WCC Publications, 1998), 122-23.

3 Ibid. Italics added.

4 *Ecumenical Mandate*, 12-15.

denominations" as possible partners or "sister communions."[5] Nevertheless, as I have pointed out, the *Mandate's* definition of ecumenism makes no reference to the goal of the unity of the churches, but only to "the unity of all believers." Does this unity include the unity of the churches? Even if so, is it then considered more important, more essential? Is "the unity of all believers," perhaps, seen as something of a higher order?

My fourth and last comment deals with another aspect of the goal of ecumenism, as described in the *Mandate's* definition. The document says that the ecumenical movement "seeks to give visible expression" to the unity at stake, a unity which all believers already "have in Jesus Christ." Here, the distinction between an invisible reality and its visible expression is introduced. Unity (of all believers) is an existing reality ("in Jesus Christ"), but it still lacks visibility. This is where ecumenism is supposed to step in. It does not have to create unity; it only has to make visible that unity that already exists invisibly. Now, we need to consider this notion very carefully. In idealistic philosophy, it is very common to make a distinction between the invisible and the visible, in such a way as to imply that the invisible is what matters and that the visible is merely an outward appearance, of secondary importance. Should that implication be avoided in our ecumenical considerations? Or does it apply to ecumenism as well? Does it really mean that ecumenism, as the movement that seeks to make visible what already exists invisibly, is *not* what matters in the first place? One could easily find this suggestion confirmed by the *Mandate's* characterization of Christian unity as in the first place "spiritual," and only in the second place "visible."[6] It is true that the document itself contains a warning. It refers to Jesus' prayer "that they all be one...so that the world may believe" (John 17:21). Jesus himself, apparently, must have had in mind "a unity that the world can see," for how else could it move

5   Ibid., 18.
6   Ibid., 7-8.

the world to believe? Therefore, "the spiritual unity of the church must never be separated from its visible expression in the institutional church." This seems to be a strong statement. Already in itself, however, it contains the distinction between "spirituality" (seen as invisibility!) and "visibility." And the question is whether the distinction as presented here contains a stimulus towards qualifying "visible unity" as of less importance than "spiritual unity." Does Jesus really need mission as an argument to make clear to his followers (as well as to realize himself) that the unity he has in mind must include visibility?[7] One might think that visibility is pretty self-evident. Apparently not so, remarkably enough, for the authors of the *Mandate*. They believe they have to argue about it.

My fourth comment is in fact closely related to the third. A unity in which churches participate cannot but be a visible unity. At least such things as pulpit and table fellowship and recognition of each other's ministries (mentioned in the *Mandate* as elements of interdenominational relationships of "full communion"[8]) will have to be officially settled. But "unity of believers," as envisaged in the *Mandate*'s definition of ecumenism, might indeed be just a "spiritual" reality, apart from or before or above any visibility. I ask again whether the *Mandate* sees the "unity of believers" as something of a higher order than a "unity of churches."

The Church Invisible: The Reformed Tradition

The view of ecumenism presented in the *Ecumenical Mandate* is not unique to that document but is to be found in the Reformed tradition at large. The distinction between "invisible unity," as

---

7 Cf. ibid., 12, where John 17:20-21 is quoted for the second time, under the heading: "Christian unity is for mission to the world."

8 Ibid., 14-15; cf. *A Formula of Agreement between the Evangelical-Lutheran Church in America, the Presbyterian Church (U.S.A.), the Reformed Church in America and the United Church of Christ on entering into full communion on the basis of A Common Calling*, in *Minutes*, 1995, 164-86 (adopted 1997 by the four respective churchwide assemblies; see *Minutes*, 1997, 186; 1998, 244-45.

something that is already a reality in Christ, and "visible unity," as a goal yet to be sought, reminds us of the distinction between the "invisible church" and the "visible church," commonly made within the Reformed tradition, especially in seventeenth- and eighteenth-century Reformed orthodoxy.[9] Heinrich Heppe, in his well-known summary of this Reformed orthodoxy, quotes the seventeenth-century Swiss Reformed theologian Johannes Henricus Heideggerus: "The church is the assembly or collection of the elect, called and believing, whom God by the Word and Spirit calls from the state of sin to the state of grace for eternal glory." Starting from this definition, the same Heideggerus cannot but come to an unambiguous statement on the church's invisibility: "The church is strictly called invisible, because we do not feel and see it as an earthly kingdom but we believe in it."[10] The emphasis on the invisibility of the church is typical of Reformed orthodoxy; Heppe quotes several other seventeenth- and eighteenth-century Reformed theologians who thought along similar lines.

Of course, this ecclesiological thinking has its impact on ecumenism. Ecclesiology and ecumenism are always interrelated. Wherever the church is considered essentially invisible, the unity of the church is considered likewise. Heppe summarizes Reformed orthodox theology on the unity of the church as follows: "The church has the character of unity...in so far as she rests on Christ as the cause of life in all believers..., and in so far as being an essentially spiritual community she is in no wise touched by the limitations natural to humanity."[11] This last argument is particularly interesting. "Essentially spiritual" over against "natural to humanity": this sounds very spiritualizing, very idealistic indeed. Here the unity of

---

[9] On what follows, see Karel Blei, *Kerk onderweg. Over Geest, Kerk en Oecumene* (Zoetermeer: Uitgeverij Boekencentrum, 1997), 91-92.

[10] Heinrich Heppe, *Reformed Dogmatics,* ed. Ernst Bizer, trans. G.T. Thomson (London: Allen and Unwin, 1950; reprinted, Grand Rapids: Baker, 1978) 657, 660.

[11] Ibid., 662.

the church seems to have become a Platonic idea, only to be revealed in heaven. In this context, there is hardly any reason to deal with a specific "question of ecumenism."

Is this particular approach to unity only a later, i.e., post-Reformation, development in the Reformed tradition? No, it is not. From the very beginning of the tradition, there are pointers in the same direction. In the Heidelberg Catechism, the well-known answer to the question, "What do you believe concerning the Holy Catholic Church?" reads as follows: "That out of the whole human race, from the beginning to the end of the world, the Son of God, by his Spirit and Word, gathers, defends, and preserves for himself unto everlasting life, a chosen communion in the unity of the true faith; and that I am, and forever shall remain, a living member of the same."[12] This, as far as I know, is the only section of the catechism in which the issue of predestination is explicitly mentioned. Whereas the Belgic Confession [13] and especially the Canons of the Synod of Dort, present the issue of predestination as a complete doctrine, here in the catechism it just stands in the background of the argument. Nevertheless, it already plays its role, in that the church is characterized as "a *chosen* community," elect unto (for) "everlasting life"; and clearly it is because of predestination that the church's members are members "forever." Here we have a foretaste of the doctrine of the perseverance of the saints, later to be developed (in continuation of Calvin's insights) in the Canons of Dort.[14] Now, predestination is essentially invisible; only the Lord knows who belongs to his communion. To the elect, assurance of belonging can only be a matter of personal faith, never a matter of general

---

12 Heidelberg Catechism, Q. 54. I use the translated text from *The Creeds of Christendom,* ed. Philip Schaff, rev. David S. Schaff (New York: Harper and Row, 1931, reprinted, Grand Rapids: Baker, 1985), 3:307-55. On this section, see Karel Blei, "Introduction," in *The Church in the Reformed Tradition,* ed. Colin E. Gunton, Páraic Reamonn, and Alan P.F. Sell, (Geneva: World Alliance of Reformed Churches, 1995), 5-7.

13 Belgic Confession (ed. Schaff [see note 12], 3:383-436), art. 16.

14 Canons of Dort (ed. Schaff, [see note 12], 3:581-97), chap. v.

observation.[15] The Heidelberg Catechism, therefore, already considers the church, "the chosen communion," as first of all an invisible reality.

Accordingly, in the catechism just as in the later tradition summarized by Heppe, there is hardly any room for a discussion of the ecumenical question; the unity of the church as such is not an issue. Unity is, of course, presupposed in the reference to "the" Holy Catholic Church, singular,[16] as gathered, defended, and preserved by the Son of God, and especially in the reference to "the unity of the true faith." The basic idea of the catechism here is that the church exists wherever true faith—understood as faith in Jesus Christ the one and only Mediator between God and humankind[17]—exists, and that there, by definition, the unity of the church is to be found. The "true faith" is the uniting factor *par excellence*. But is it really so? Church history, alas, demonstrates otherwise. The "true faith" became the object of different interpretations, of heavy and bitter discussions. Confessors of the "true faith" became defenders of that faith, fighters for that faith. Passion for the "true faith" broke communions apart. Who is entitled to claim the right understanding of "true faith"? In fact, the Reformed tend to be unwilling, as individuals, to leave that claim to anyone other than themselves.

The catechism's reference to "the unity of true faith" presupposes that faith precedes church (and church unity). Where faith is seen as first and foremost an individual, inner reality, a reality experienced and fostered in the personal heart, there this phrase implies that the individual believers are first, and the church, the communion (better: the sum) of believers is second. This, to a large extent, has

---

15 See Canons of Dort, I.12; cf. Heidelberg Catechism, Q. 86.
16 The Apostles' Creed, on which the Heidelberg Catechism bases its exposition of Christian faith (see Q. 23), unlike the Nicene-Constantinopolitan Creed, does not contain the word *una* ("one") as a cardinal number before *ecclesia* ("church").
17 Heidelberg Catechism, Q. 21 and Q. 60. The Belgic Confession, art. 27, calls the church "a holy congregation and assembly of true Christian believers, expecting all their salvation in Jesus Christ."

been common Reformed understanding indeed. The result is that, even among the Reformed themselves, church unity was broken exactly because of the desire to maintain the truth of faith. Thus Reformed ecclesiological thinking has tended to invoke the unity of the church only when it was needed "to balance the budget."

The Church Visible: The Roman Catholic Tradition

To a large extent, Reformed ecclesiology has been developed *vis-a-vis* Roman Catholicism. Roman Catholic ecclesiology does not know of any "essential" invisibility of the church at the expense of its visibility. On the contrary, here the church of Christ, the church of the Creed, is considered essentially visible, namely in the church as it is (visibly!) governed and guided by pope and bishops, as the successors to Peter and the other apostles. It is, in other words, visible precisely in the Roman Catholic Church itself. It is this idea of obvious visibility that the Reformed tradition has had in mind when it has focused primarily on the invisibility of the church. We have to say a few more things about that.

Over the centuries, Roman Catholic ecclesiology has been very consistent in this assertion of the essential visibility of the church. It is true that *Lumen Gentium,* the Second Vatican Council's Dogmatic Constitution on the Church, avoided a strict identification of the church of Christ, that is, the church of the apostles, with "the Catholic Church, which is governed by the successor of Peter and by the bishops in communion with him." As a result of a modification of the original text that was introduced at the very last moment, *Lumen Gentium* does not state that the church of Christ "is" the Catholic Church, but rather that the church of Christ "subsists in" the Catholic Church. Thus it leaves room for recognition that even outside the Catholic Church, i.e. "outside its visible confines," there are "many elements of sanctification and of truth," as "gifts belonging to the church of Christ" and therefore as "forces impelling towards Catholic unity."[18] This wording at least *seems* to

18 *Lumen Gentium*, par. 8. Text, trans. Colman O'Neill, O.P., in Austin P. Flannery, ed., *Documents of Vatican II* (Grand Rapids: Eerdmans, 1975), 350-426.

avoid a strict identification. But careful observation indicates otherwise. The wording does not deny the identification but only qualifies it. The word "subsisting" contains a notion of continuity in time. It draws attention to the fact that Vatican II does not regard the church of Christ as something ideal, something "up there," that would then have found its realization here on earth (in the concrete Roman Catholic Church). The Vatican Council states here, instead, that from its beginning the (confessed, believed) church of Christ has been a historical reality. It is this historical reality that is said today to "subsist" in the Roman Catholic Church—an assertion that is, of course, fully in agreement with Roman Catholic tradition.[19]

Then what about Roman Catholic ecumenism? Since Vatican II, the Roman Catholic Church has indeed presented itself as a participant in the ecumenical movement. On the very same day as the council issued *Lumen Gentium*, it also issued its Decree on Ecumenism, *Unitatis redintegratio*. Here, mention is made of "the separated churches and communities" as "by no means deprived of significance and importance in the mystery of salvation" because "the Spirit of Christ has not refrained from using them as means of salvation." In the matter of Roman Catholic judgment of these other churches, this was an important breakthrough, and in the intervening years official papal statements have confirmed this ecumenical openness. Pope John Paul II explicitly did so in his encyclical letter *Ut unum sint*, published in 1995, which is a clear witness to this pope's passion for unity.

For what unity? For the "unity of all believers," the ecumenical goal fostered in the Reformed tradition? For the "unity of the churches," the ecumenical goal envisaged in the context of the

---

19 Cf. Karel Blei, "Participating Together in the One Church of Christ," in *From Roots to Fruits. Protestants and Catholics Towards a Common Understanding of the Church*, ed. Martin E. Brinkman and Henk Witte (Geneva: World Alliance of Reformed Churches, 1998), 128-29, 133-34 (with reference to, *inter alia,* Francis A. Sullivan, S.J., "'Subsistit in': The Significance of Vatican II's Doctrine of the Church of Christ not that it 'is' but that it 'subsists in' the Roman Catholic Church," in *One in Christ* 22 [1986]: 115-123.)

World Council of Churches? No, the Roman Catholic Church, even today, under the pontificate of Pope John Paul II, has a different understanding of ecumenism. In the encyclical *Ut unum sint* as so often before, the papal pontificate itself is presented as the indispensable "ministry of unity," to be recognized as such by all Christians and churches. Differences in liturgy, in church structure, etc., it is said, may exist and are not, in themselves, hindrances of real church unity, provided a common recognition of papal primacy also exists. Such was the case, the pope states, during the first millennium, and he passionately desires it to be so again now, at the beginning of the third. To help make that possible, the pope declares himself willing to engage in dialogue, not on the principle of the papal primacy (the "Petrine ministry of unity") as such, but rather on the way in which it is practiced. The primacy as such will have to be recognized but could be executed in a different style.[20] Is this one more call to return to the Roman Catholic mother church? More cautiously, let us say that it is a call to return to that unity that, as the pope sees it, existed during the first millennium.

To Roman Catholicism, unity, like the church itself, is not something presently invisible that will be made visible in and through the ecumenical movement, as the Reformed Church's *Ecumenical Mandate* would have it. Neither is unity a matter of hope, to which the different churches are calling each other in the context of the ecumenical movement, as the present World Council Constitution understands it. Rather, unity exists and is visible, today as it has always existed, in the Roman Catholic Church itself, the only church that is fully entitled to bear the name of "church." In agreement with the Vatican II Decree on Ecumenism, the recent declaration *Dominus Iesus*, issued in August 2000 by the Roman Catholic Congregation for the Doctrine of the Faith, points out that other "churches" are at best "true particular churches." That is the case with the eastern churches, because of their preservation of "the

20 On *Ut unum sint,* see Blei, *Kerk onderweg,* 134-35.

valid episcopate"—in the apostolic succession—and so the "valid Eucharist." The other "ecclesial communities" may call themselves "church," but they "are not churches in the proper sense of the word."21 Although this wording does not literally occur in the Vatican II Decree on Ecumenism, it does not contradict the doctrine of Vatican II. I have already quoted the statement in *Lumen Gentium* that the "elements of sanctification and of truth" that exist outside the Catholic Church are "forces impelling towards Catholic unity." This means that their existence outside the Catholic Church, strictly speaking, is an anomaly, almost an "impossible possibility," for these elements essentially have their place *within* the Catholic Church. That is where they belong. *Dominus Iesus* warns us not to misunderstand the assertion of *Lumen Gentium* that the church of Christ "subsists in" the Catholic Church. That phrase certainly does not imply "that the one church of Christ could subsist also in non-Catholic churches and ecclesial communities." Instead, "the council...chose the word *subsistit* precisely to clarify that there exists only one 'subsistence' of the true church." 22 This statement is, to be sure, an interpretation of *Lumen Gentium* by the Congregation for the Doctrine of the Faith, and it makes reference to an earlier pronouncement of its own to the same effect.23 The congregation is here closing a gap that was left open by the council. (The congregation, indeed, is always inclined to draw sharp lines, whereas ecumenists, even Roman Catholic ecumenists, rather like to avoid doing so.) Nonetheless, it is difficult to deny that the congregation's interpretation concurs with the meaning of *Lumen Gentium*. The interpretation, anyway, makes it crystal clear—if it were not yet already clear—that to Roman Catholicism ecumenism cannot be a

---

21 *Dominus Iesus* (Rome: Congregation on the Doctrine of the Faith, 2000), pars. 16-17.
22 *Dominus Iesus*, note 56.
23 With reference to the book, *Church, Charism and Power,* by Leonardo Boff (1985).

movement of churches (plural) *towards* (common) visible unity. It rather presupposes that that unity exists already in full visibility.

Tensions of History: Roman and Reformed Ecclesiologies

Of course, the Roman Catholic Church today is not quite the same church as that of the sixteenth century. In the time of the Reformation, today's plurality of churches (denominations) did not yet exist in western Christianity. There was therefore no reason for Roman Catholic ecclesiology to emphasize a difference between the true church and other *so-called* "churches." One could even say that a real ecclesiology as such, in the systematic sense of the word, had not been developed, since it was not yet needed. Only after, and because of, the Reformation was Roman Catholicism forced to develop its own basic ecclesiological ideas systematically. [24]

These ideas, however, did not arrive out of the blue. They only made explicit what had already been implicit in Roman Catholic theology and church life over the centuries. Already in the time of the Reformation, it was a basic Roman Catholic conviction that the church, governed by pope and bishops, was in direct historical continuity, through apostolic succession, with the church of the apostles. And it was exactly this conviction that the Reformers felt compelled to question.[25] They expressed their criticism of both the practice and the doctrine of the Roman Catholic Church, to which they themselves originally belonged and within which they themselves had been baptized—a criticism based on their own reading of the gospel. They did so the more vigorously as they experienced that their own understanding of the gospel was not accepted in the church. To the Reformers, the fact that the alleged actual, visible reality of the church was presented as the decisive argument against them rendered any serious consideration of their

---

24 Cf. *Towards a Common Understanding of the Church. Reformed/Roman Catholic International Dialogue: Second Phase, 1984-1990* (Geneva: World Alliance of Reformed Churches, 1991), 13-14.
25 On what follows, see Blei, *Kerk onderweg*, 89-90.

criticism impossible from the outset and meant that a rupture could no longer be avoided.

The Reformers were compelled, therefore, to make explicit their own rejection of precisely this Roman Catholic appeal to visible church reality as such. That is what John Calvin is doing in the chapter of his *Institutes* in which he distinguishes the "true church" from the "false church." In discussing the "false church" he does not hesitate to point to what he calls the "Papists" or "Romanists." They, he says, "give us the most magnificent commendations of their church to make us believe that there is no other in the world...But by what reason do they prove theirs to be the true church? They allege from ancient records what formerly occurred in Italy, in France, in Spain; that they are descended from these holy men, who by sound doctrine founded and raised the churches in these countries, and confirmed their doctrine and the edification of the church by their blood; and that the church...has been preserved by a perpetual succession of bishops, that it might never be lost." But this appeal to "ancient records" and "a perpetual succession of bishops" is a "vain pretence, unless the truth of Christ, which was transmitted from the fathers, be permanently retained pure and uncorrupted by their posterity."[26] The visibility to which they appeal may be impressive, but if "we cannot discover" there "the Word of God," this visibility is just "vain glitter." Whether or not the church of Christ is present cannot be answered merely by reference to an impressive proof of historical succession or of continuity. The church is founded "upon the 'doctrine of the apostles and prophets.'" and upon nothing else.[27] It "is preserved by two bonds—agreement in sound doctrine and brotherly love." But in the end, the second is dependent upon the first. The "union

---

[26] John Calvin, *Institutes of the Christian Religion*, IV.2.2. I use the text as translated by John Allen (Philadelphia: Presbyterian Board of Publication, 1936).
[27] Calvin, *Institutes*, IV.2.4.

of affection" is itself "dependent on the unity of faith, as its foundation, end, and rule."[28]

The "unity of faith": here we find, in Calvin's *Institutes*, the same expression we found earlier in the Heidelberg Catechism. But does this phrase really mean what we thought? In my discussion of the catechism, I pointed to the possibility that the "true faith," which according to the catechism constitutes the foundation of the church's unity, is an inner reality experienced and fostered in the heart of the individual believer. There is no doubt that among Reformed people it has often been understood that way. There is, however, another possibility, namely that the "true faith" is not so much "my" faith as "the" faith, which comes *to* us (and *to* me, as belonging to that "us") from the apostles, from the gospel, handed over to us (to me) by those who preceded us, and who, together with us (with me) belong to the church. In that case, it is not we who confess and carry faith; rather, it is faith that carries us. "Faith" is in this sense another word for the gospel itself—the gospel *as* confessed in faith. True faith, interpreted this way, is larger, richer, deeper than we ourselves can grasp. We need each other in the church to understand it more adequately. Seen in this perspective, it appears inappropriate to state (as is often done in Reformed circles) that the individual believer comes first and the church second. Even among Reformed it is feasible, even obvious, to reverse the order so as to state that the church, the communion, comes first, and the individual believer owes his or her existence as a believer to the church, just as the members of the body derive their living existence from the body and cannot live without being connected to it (cf. 1 Cor.12).

I do not know whether such a notion of the relation of individual to church is within the intention of the catechism. But I do think that this is what Calvin had in mind. In the statements quoted above from the *Institutes*, we hear of the church not only as a "unity of faith," but also as that which is founded "upon 'the doctrine of

28 Calvin, *Institutes*, IV.2.5.

apostles and prophets,'" and as the place where "the Word of God" can be discovered and where "the truth of Christ" has been "permanently retained pure and uncorrupted." All these expressions stand on one line, parallel, and with the same apparent meaning. When writing of "faith" as uniting factor for the church, Calvin does not understand it as a personal, individual act or attitude (*fides qua*, the faith *by which* I believe); rather he refers to the *content* of faith (*fides quae*, the faith *which* I believe). It is that content which can also be called "the doctrine of apostles and prophets," or "the Word of God," or "the truth of Christ." Just so, the "truth of Christ," as Calvin says, was "transmitted from the fathers"; we did not invent it ourselves, but received it. Thus Calvin himself refers to a historical process of continuity—a process of transmission, of handing over, from the former generations (the "fathers") to their "posterity."

Therefore, we need not be surprised when we find, in Calvin's expression of his ecclesiological ideas, reference to the church as "mother" of the believers. "There is no other way of entrance into life, unless we are conceived by her, born of her, nourished at her breast, and continually preserved under her care and government, till we are divested of this mortal flesh, and 'become like the angels.' For our infirmity will not admit of our dismission from her school; we must continue under her instruction and discipline to the end of our lives...[O]ut of her bosom there can be no hope of remission of sins, or any salvation...."[29]

Two things are very clear here. First, Calvin apparently does not think that the believers, by coming together, "make" the church; it is rather the church that, humanly speaking, makes the believers. This reminds us of the well-known statement by the third-century church father Cyprian: "You cannot have God for your Father if you have not the Church for your Mother."[30] Second, the church

---

[29] Calvin, *Institutes*, IV.1.4.
[30] Cyprian, *The Unity of the Catholic Church*, chap. 6 (trans. Maurice Bévenot [New York: Newman Press, 1956], 48-49).

to which Calvin refers here is the *visible* church, as is implied by the "mother" metaphor itself. An invisible mother would be of little use to her children!

It is true that Calvin also speaks of the invisibility of the church insofar as it founded upon God's secret election.[31] But in his ecclesiological argument, his main emphasis is undoubtedly upon the church as a visible reality. That is obvious already in the very heading of Book IV of his *Institutes*, the portion of the work that contains his discussion of the church: "On the external means or aids by which God calls us into communion with Christ, and retains us in it." As one of these "external means"—indeed as the first among them—the church can hardly be just invisible.

Is this another Calvin? No, it is the same Calvin, who is now, however, engaged in another controversy, namely the controversy with the Anabaptists, who (as Calvin saw them) claimed to be guided directly by the Holy Spirit and therefore to be able to do without the visible church.[32] In developing his own ecclesiological thinking, Calvin felt challenged not only by Roman Catholicism, but also by Anabaptism. It was *vis-a-vis* the Anabaptists that he spoke of the church as becoming visible, not (as Roman Catholicism argues) in any historical continuity as such, and not in the formal existence of an episcopal ministry that claims to be in apostolic succession, but in the pure administration of Word and sacraments. The church is there to be seen where it actually happens that the Word of God is purely preached and heard and the sacraments of baptism and Holy Supper are administered according to the institution of Christ. These are "the marks by which the church is to be distinguished."[33] Sharp is Calvin's criticism of those who, "from a false notion of perfect sanctity," separate themselves from that visible and true church. They may be right in perceiving within that church a lack of "perfect purity and integrity of life," or even

[31] Calvin, *Institutes*, IV.1.2.
[32] Calvin, *Institutes*, IV.1.6, 11-13.
[33] Calvin, *Institutes*, IV.1. 9-10.

in discovering faults in the preaching of the doctrine or the administration of the sacraments. But in that case it should be realized that "all the articles of the true doctrine are not of the same description," and that not every controversy necessarily destroys the unity of the faith. Anyway, such perception or discovery of faults in the church should never be a reason to leave the church. "We ought not, on account of every trivial difference of sentiment, to abandon the church." [34]

Real Unity in Reformed Perspective

Such were Calvin's thoughts on ecclesiology as they bear upon our topic. These have been influential in the Reformed tradition. In the Belgic Confession, for example, we find basically the same two lines of thinking as in Calvin: first, the distinction between the "true church" and the "false church" (as a critique of Roman Catholicism), and second, the same ideas on "the marks of the true church," and on the necessity of being and remaining a member of that church (as a critique of that separatism Calvin identified with Anabaptism).[35]

We may well state that in later Reformed orthodoxy (seventeenth and eighteenth centuries) the second line of thought, with its emphasis on the visibility of the church, had to a large extent been forgotten. That is why the Reformed are always inclined to underestimate the seriousness of the ecumenical question. They always like to think that ecumenism is only a matter of making visible the unity that already exists invisibly in Christ. I opened this essay by pointing out that very tendency in the *Ecumenical Mandate* document, in its definition of ecumenism. Let me now, in contrast, state bluntly that an "invisible unity" by definition is *not* a "unity in Christ," however Christian it may be, because Jesus Christ himself did not become *invisible* man. There is reason to re-emphasize the second line of thought.

---

[34] Calvin, *Institutes*, IV.1.12-13.
[35] Belgic Confession, arts. 28-29.

In Reformed perspective, ecumenism will always have to take seriously the present, shameful reality of divided churches. That reality prevents us from being able to claim "our" church to be "the" church of Christ on earth. At the same time, we cannot give up our faith that we find Christ's church represented in "our" church—that "our" church is indeed rightly called "church," because in it we find the true preaching of the Word and the true administration of the sacraments. Yet do we then deny the name of "church" to all other communities and denominations? Are we so sure that in other denominations Word and sacraments are not administered as adequately as in ours, or at least adequately enough? Is there not elsewhere in Christianity openness to dimensions of the gospel and of church life that we ourselves have not yet discovered, but of which we should take account? If so, then we cannot accept the present situation of divided churches. Therefore, Calvin's warning against unjust separation is once more timely and urgent, although in a sense that he did not specifically have in mind—namely, as a criticism of easy denominationalism.

The Reformed do not think that church unity can be achieved just by returning to a lost past, or by sticking to historical continuity as such. For that, they consider the living proclamation of the Word and the living administration of the sacraments—I could also say, the living reality of the Holy Spirit—too important, too powerful. Real church unity, in our Reformed understanding, does not lie behind us, so as to make us turn backward. It rather lies before us. It is what Christ has in store for us. As such, however, already now it needs to be our point of orientation. Ecumenism in Reformed perspective means being church *en route*, on the move, looking forward, as Abraham did, "to the city which has foundations whose architect and builder is God" (Hebrews 11:10). It means knowing that we have not yet arrived.

5

Full Communion: What's the Buzz?

Douglas Fromm

In 1997, the General Synod of the Reformed Church in America (RCA) voted to enter into full communion with the Evangelical Lutheran Church in America (ELCA) under the terms of the Reformed/Lutheran *Formula of Agreement*.[1] Other Reformed churches signing this landmark agreement were the Presbyterian Church (USA) and the United Church of Christ. Ever since, the RCA has been abuzz with the effects of that decision on its identity, mission, vision, life, and ministry.

Part of the buzz has been fearful and at times somewhat angry. From the outset, anxious concern spread rapidly about our partners in the agreement, particularly one of our sister churches on the Reformed side, the United Church of Christ (UCC). There were fears that our denomination would be compromised by an unbiblical attitude toward homosexuality and anti-Trinitarian influences. As a result, the General Synods of 1998, 1999, and 2000 received overtures calling for a range of actions, from admonition of the UCC to a dismantling of the *Formula of Agreement*.

---

[1] *Minutes of the General Synod of the RCA* (hereafter, *Minutes*), 1997, 186.

70

The overtures to the General Synod of 1998 called for the suspension of RCA relationship with the United Church of Christ, a withdrawal from the RCA relationship of full communion with the UCC, and the severance of ties with the UCC. The synod denied these overtures.[2]

The General Synod of 1999 received an overture that called for the general secretary to communicate a warning to the General Council of the United Church of Christ that the RCA would sever all ties unless the UCC repented of and changed its "affirmation of practicing homosexual and bisexual lifestyles as appropriate for Christians." The overture was denied by the synod.[3] A second overture raised a new concern about the UCC, that of its relation to Unitarianism. The General Synod denied the overture.[4] At the synods of 1998 and 1999, there was an unusually high level of interest in the Advisory Committee on Christian Unity, especially on the part of delegates wishing to weight its membership toward support of the overtures.

The General Synod of 2000 received an overture from the classes of California, Canadian Prairies, Central California, Central Iowa, Illiana, South Grand Rapids, Rocky Mountains, and Zeeland requesting that the RCA begin a process of separation from the United Church of Christ. In response to the overture, the General Synod voted to adopt a statement that clarified the RCA understanding of the *Formula of Agreement* and the boundaries of its relationship with the United Church of Christ and the ruling out of any new cooperation with the UCC.[5] This action was to be communicated by a letter sent to all congregations of the RCA making clear that the RCA "will not intentionally pursue a closer ecumenical relationship with the UCC beyond that which exists through a common membership in councils of Churches...and

2   *Minutes,* 1998, 250-252.
3   *Minutes,* 1999, 185.
4   Ibid., 186
5   *Minutes,* 2000, 113-14.

currently existing cooperative engagements...."[6] This action appears to have reduced the anxieties. I am pleased to say that the synod of 2001 received no overtures on the *Formula*. The fearful and sometimes angry buzz has quieted.

In another sense, the RCA remains abuzz with the effects of the 1997 decision. For from the outset, and even when the debates about our relations with the UCC were raging, the *Formula* has been generating a flurry of cooperative activity at every level of the denomination—and that activity continues strong.

So what is happening? Here is an overview. (Let me be sure to note there that in all of the activities I shall mention, the RCA adheres to the stipulations of the above-mentioned action of the General Synod of 2000.)

In *oversight*, a coordinating committee monitors what is happening as a result of the agreement and refers matters of program to the appropriate units of the participating churches. Following their respective votes on the *Formula* in 1997, the four partner churches formed this committee to ensure that the commitments would be carried out. It consists of twelve members, including one clergyperson, one layperson, and one ecumenical staff person from each church, all appointed by the respective heads of communion.

In *global ministries*, staff members of the four churches meet to discuss and discern matters of common interest. So far, they have discussed joint ministries in the Middle East and Southeast Asia, programs for interfaith relations, and issues concerning the preparation, identity, and role of mission personnel today.

In *multi-cultural ministries*, a program called "CARE Partners" has been established. CARE stands for "Communion Agreement Racial Ethnic." The program explores networking and shared mission. It enables cooperation in the development of resources on multicultural sensitivity and plans joint training events for leaders and staff. "CARE Partners" is currently working on a strategy for

6   Ibid., 113.

developing new churches in racial/ethnic communities, to be recommended to each of the four churches with the goal of collaboration instead of competition. The group encourages mutual nurture and support among the partners, develops a master calendar of events, works on strategies for liberation and wholeness rooted in spirituality, and pools resources of many kinds—human, literary, cultural, narrative, homiletic, physical, and historical—for use across what were formerly uncrossed boundaries.

In the area of *communications*, staff persons have met to discuss possible joint ventures. One idea is to produce a joint brochure that would profile each of the four churches in a way that is easy for congregations to use. Another idea is to produce a video highlighting the ministry and mission of each church; still another is to undertake joint promotion of the resources that the individual churches produce separately.

In the area of *ordained ministry,* the *Formula* declared the four churches' agreement "to recognize each others' various ministries and make provision for the orderly exchange of ordained ministers of Word and sacrament."[7] A cooperative team has produced a manual, *The Orderly Exchange of Ministers Of Word And Sacrament: Principles, Policies, and Procedures,*[8] which summarizes each church's procedures concerning calls, installations, contracts, and oversight and includes a list of frequently asked questions. And already, clergy are providing leadership and pastoral care across denominational lines. For example, the First Presbyterian Church and the Christ Lutheran Church in Ridgefield Park, New Jersey, now share the services of a full-time pastor whom neither congregation could have supported by itself. Another example: an RCA minister, Diane Konynenbelt, serves under extended appointment as pastor of the St. Stephen Evangelical Lutheran Church in Rockford, Michigan, where, according to a recent article in the Grand Rapids *Press*, the

---

7   *A Formula of Agreement*, in *Minutes,* 1995, 164.
8   (Louisville: Office of the General Assembly, Presbyterian Church [USA], 2000).

congregation has been pleased with her understanding of Lutheran tradition.[9]

Projects in *education* are also under way. Seminary professors from the four churches, including Professor Leanne Van Dyk of Western Theological Seminary, came together in a consultation in Geneva, Switzerland, in the summer of 2001 to consider theological education from an ecumenical perspective. In the area around Albany, New York, a "Capital District Theological Committee" of representatives from *Formula* churches and seminaries (Auburn, Andover Newton, Philadelphia Lutheran, and New Brunswick) is working to create a program of continuing education for clergy and laity.

The four churches are also making *mutual appointments*. RCA representatives now serve on the Ecumenical Relations Committee of the UPUSA, the Executive Council of the UCC, and the Church Council of the ELCA. They are full members of those bodies with all rights and privileges. In 2001 the General Synod adopted the first reading of a change in its by-laws to include a nonvoting representative of the ELCA on the General Synod Council.[10] The General Synod Commissions on Christian Unity, Theology, and Christian Action will also include representatives from the other churches of the *Formula*.

In *worship,* national, regional, and local eucharistic celebrations have been held from California to New York, from Texas to Michigan.

Much, therefore, has been happening since that historic vote of 1997, when the RCA took the first step of saying yes to this new ecumenical initiative. In a letter to my office, one RCA pastor seemed to say it all when he wrote, "The passage of the *Formula of Agreement* establishing full communion has given us permission to work together and even prods us to do so. It has been a great and wonderful gift to the churches."

---

9   Elizabeth Slowick, "She's Reformed, but she leads a Lutheran church," Grand Rapids *Press*, 16 December 2000, B1.
10 *Minutes*, 2001, 73.

With all this in mind, I want to close by reflecting on the gift that our four churches have given, not just to each other but to the Church Catholic and to the ecumenical endeavor.

A Common Calling, the document that preceded and inspired the *Formula of Agreement,* points out that the Reformed/Lutheran dialogue offers a new logic of ecumenical conversation. Previous dialogues employed a conditional logic. The language was one of *"if...then."* *If* we find agreement, *then* we can move forward toward unity. *If* dialogue partners find consensus on theological issues, on ecclesial issues, on sacraments, on orders of ministry, on the locus of authority in the church, *then* we can move forward and talk of full communion and ecumenical cooperation. The new logic is expressed in the language of *"because...therefore." Because* we find agreement on certain issues, items, etc., *therefore* we ought to "exercise our common calling in witness and service to the world."[11] The centerpiece of such a logic or method of dialogue is to be found in the concept of "mutual affirmation and admonition"—an imaginative concept which has moved conversations forward in spite of the remaining differences. It is a concept that enables churches that differ in significant ways to join together, giving testimony to their common faith and desire without masking the differences and distinctions. Distinctiveness appears then as a gift to the church, rather than an obstacle to unity—the natural result of sincere efforts to be faithful to the gospel within different historical contexts. The principle of mutual affirmation and admonition "allows for the affirmation of agreement while at the same time allowing a process of mutual edification and correction in areas where there is not total agreement. Each tradition brings its 'corrective witness' to the other while fostering continuing theological reflection and dialogue to further clarify the unity of faith they share and seek,"[12] thus serving the life

11 *A Common Calling: The Witness of Our Reformation Churches in North America Today. The Report of the Lutheran-Reformed Committee for Theological Conversations, 1988-1992,* ed. Keith F. Nickle and Timothy F. Lull (Minneapolis: Augsburg Fortress, 1993), 57.

12 *A Formula of Agreement,* 166.

and mission of the church. "The theological diversity within our common confession provides both the complementarity needed for a full and adequate witness to the gospel (mutual affirmation) and the corrective reminder that every theological approach is a partial and incomplete witness to the gospel (mutual admonition)."[13] Each needs the other for their shared witness, that all "may be one...that the world may believe (John 17:21)."

In the fall of 1996, a group of concerned RCA pastors gathered at the Stony Point Conference Center in New York. All were concerned about the movement of the RCA in what one participant termed "a more conservative, less tolerant direction." Speakers addressed several topics, ranging from church order to ecumenism. I was asked to speak on the then-upcoming General Synod vote on full communion. In concluding my remarks that day I said: "The Reformed Church in America will be the first church to vote. It is not hyperbole to say that the worldwide church will be watching us. We have an opportunity to send a signal that the Lutheran-Reformed breach is ended and that heirs of the Reformation can live and work together, that they can address contemporary issues of faith, society, and culture with a hermeneutic of truth spoken in love, rather than the old hermeneutic of suspicion, polemics, and division. We have an opportunity to close this century with a positive step into the next. The vote will be a defining moment for the RCA. A positive vote will affirm the living out of our *Ecumenical Mandate* of 1996 and our statements of 1981 and 1966.[14] It will make the principle of 'mutual affirmation and admonition' a new model for theological reflection in ecumenical dialogue everywhere."

I am pleased to affirm that this old, sometimes stubborn, feisty, quarrelsome, and yet grace-filled church of ours lived up to the challenge given by the One who prayed for us, long before we even knew him.

---

[13] *A Common Calling*, 66.
[14] *Minutes,* 1996, 197 (text: 1995, 174-86); 1981, 146-47; 1966, 246-47.

6

Dominus Iesus: A Stumbling Block to Reformed-Catholic Dialogue?

Dennis Tamburello, O.F.M.

Introduction

My own critical reaction to *Dominus Iesus,* the statement of 6 August 2000 from the Congregation for the Doctrine of the Faith, can be summarized in the following two vignettes, which I will return to later in this essay:

1. Charles Schulz once drew a *Peanuts* cartoon in which Snoopy tells us that he is writing a book about theology. He has decided to call it, "Has it ever occurred to you that you might be wrong?"
2. I once heard a story about a theology professor who began and ended all of his theology courses by putting the following statement on the blackboard: *Deus mysterium est:* God is a mystery.

I hope you will forgive me if I speak not only of Reformed-Roman Catholic dialogue but also of some of the broader issues raised by *Dominus Iesus* that are relevant for all Christians. However, the main question that I shall address is this: is this document, which defends "the unicity and salvific universality of Jesus Christ and the Church," a stumbling block to Reformed-Catholic dialogue?

The short answer is yes—but I will argue that it doesn't have to be fatal.

Reaction to the document's publication was swift and sharp. From the Catholic side, the Swiss priest and theologian Hans Küng, never one to mince words, branded it "a mixture of medieval backwardness and Vatican megalomania." The *Tablet* of London more mercifully described it as "a public relations disaster....What a pity that it sounds notes of triumphalism that the sympathetic style and way of acting of Pope John XXIII, newly beatified, seemed to have dispelled forever."[1]

From the Reformed side, the Reverend Dr. Setri Nyomi, the newly elected general secretary of the World Alliance of Reformed Churches, had this to say in a letter dated 8 September 2000, to Cardinal Edward Cassidy of the Pontifical Council for Promoting Christian Unity:

> This declaration seems to go against the spirit of Vatican II, as we understand it, and the progress made in relationships and dialogues since then. Vatican II, in our understanding, opened up many possibilities of relationship which had been closed before. On the other hand, we see *Dominus Iesus* as part of a sustained effort by Catholic conservatives to deny the growing relationship and respect between and among the different ecclesial communities. While we respect many elements of the declaration, we are most concerned about the statement on when a church is a proper church and when it is not. This concern relates also to the letter from your colleague Cardinal Ratzinger on the use of the term "sister churches.". . .

---

[1] Quoted in Edmund Doogue and Stephen Brown, "*Dominus Iesus* a 'Public Relations Disaster' for Ecumenism, Say Critics," in *Christianity Today*, 11 September 2000. This article appears to be available only online at ChristianityToday.com, <http://www.christianitytoday.com/ct/2000/137/34.0.html>.

As in the spirit and letter of Vatican II, we await your clarification on whether or not we are still to believe that the Roman Catholic Church takes seriously the "special affinity and close relationship" (Decree on Ecumenism, 19) binding the Roman Catholic Church to Protestant churches.

...In spite of our dismay, the World Alliance of Reformed Churches remains committed to dialogue with you.[2]

Dr. Nyomi's letter gives us reason to hope that fruitful dialogue will continue, despite the damage caused by *Dominus Iesus*. I, for one, am grateful that at least some in the Reformed community are willing to give us the benefit of the doubt. With all of this as a backdrop, I offer my own tentative reflections.

The Bigger Picture: Interfaith Dialogue

I would suggest that the bigger concern that arises from this document is not Reformed-Catholic dialogue but interfaith dialogue. Since this concern is relevant to all of us, I would like to begin with some comments on this point.

On the positive side, let us acknowledge that Christians *should* assert the "definitive and complete character of the revelation of Jesus Christ." [3] I do not think that we really help interfaith dialogue by putting aside or minimizing the centrality of our conviction that Jesus Christ is the savior of the world. I believe that if Jesus is who we say he is, if God truly became incarnate in the particular human being Jesus of Nazareth, then this *must* be significant for every human being who ever lived, whether they have heard of him or not.

This conviction is what is behind a notion like Karl Rahner's "anonymous Christianity," the idea that anyone who lives an

---

2 Letter to Cardinal Cassidy, quoted from World Alliance of Reformed Churches website, <http://www.warc.ch/2000/16.html>.

3 Congregation for the Doctrine of the Faith, *Dominus Iesus*, official English translation of the Vatican document, published in *Origins*, vol. 30, no. 14 (14 September 2000), paragraph 5.

authentic spiritual life has a kind of implicit connection with Jesus.[4] But when I learned about this in seminary, my professor explained that Rahner intended this to be an "in-house" expression: one that Christians should use to reinforce *each other's* faith in Jesus as the definitive revelation of God, *not* as an argument to be brought forward in interfaith dialogue. However, in-house expressions have a way of leaking out and becoming part of the public discussion, and Rahner's "anonymous Christianity" has provoked much critical response.

Having said that we must hold fast to *our* convictions as Christians, I would add that we should fully expect people of other religious traditions to hold fast to theirs. I do not see how there can be any real dialogue if the particular beliefs, doctrines, and practices of different faith traditions are not taken seriously. In this connection, I would criticize John Hick's well-known three theological options for interfaith dialogue: exclusivism, inclusivism, and pluralism. [5] In my view, Hick calls for an approach to dialogue that reduces religious experience to a lowest common denominator and simply dismisses any claims to distinctiveness. I am more receptive to the views of scholars such as Francis Clooney and James Fredericks, who argue that comparative study of other traditions, rather than comparative judgments, should be our goal. [6]

4   For a fuller treatment of the notion of "anonymous Christianity," see Karl Rahner, "Anonymous Christianity," in *Concerning Vatican Council II*, vol. 6 of *Theological Investigations*, trans. Karl-H. and Boniface Kruger (Baltimore: Helicon Press, 1969), 390-98; and "Observations on the Problem of the 'Anonymous Christian,'" in *Ecclesiology; Questions in the Church; The Church in the World*, vol. 14 of *Theological Investigations*, trans. David Bourke (New York: Seabury, 1976), 280-94.

5   See John Hick, "The Non-Absoluteness of Christianity," in John Hick and Paul Knitter, eds., *The Myth of Christian Uniqueness: Toward a Pluralistic Theology* (Maryknoll: Orbis Books, 1987), 16-36.

6   James L. Fredericks, *Faith Among Faiths: Christian Theology and Non-Christian Religions* (New York: Paulist Press, 1999), especially chap. 7, 139-61; and Francis X. Clooney, "The Study of Non-Christian Religions in the Post-Vatican II Roman Catholic Church," *Journal of Ecumenical Studies* 28:3 (1991): 482-94.

In my opinion, our dialogue with other faiths should be conducted with the awareness, as described in the *Peanuts* vignette above, that *we might be wrong*. Please do not misunderstand me. I do not think we *are* wrong. I think our convictions about Christ and Christianity are basically correct. But we need to take seriously the "if" I referred to a few paragraphs ago: "if" Jesus is who we say he is, etc. *Dominus Iesus* needs to take more seriously its own assertion that "the depth of the divine mystery *in itself* remains transcendent and inexhaustible.[7]

It *would* be wonderful if we could know definitively that there is no "salvific action of God beyond the unique mediation of Christ,"[8] but if we could know that, then we would not have faith, but scientific certitude. As scripture says, "It is better to fear God than men" (Acts 5:29—and I do mean *men* in this case!) Even Cardinal Ratzinger cannot give me the audacity to presume to tell God what the limits of his or her "salvific action" are. As that theology teacher once said, and as *Dominus Iesus* itself affirms, "Deus mysterium est."

We cannot have it both ways. We cannot insist that God is a mystery, and in the same breath claim that God must act within the boundaries that we, with our limited perspective, can identify. While the framers of *Dominus Iesus* surely did not intend to imply this, the language of the document leaves it open to precisely this misunderstanding.

A Buddhist once spoke to Karl Rahner and asked him how he would feel about being called an "anonymous Buddhist." Rahner was perfectly comfortable with this designation. In saying this, he wasn't giving away anything of his Christian convictions; but he was recognizing that ultimate reality cannot be contained in any one set of categories, including those of Christianity.

The Issue for Reformed-Catholic Relations

The crux of the issue for Reformed-Catholic relations can be found in paragraph 17 of *Dominus Iesus*, which states:

7 *Dominus Iesus*, par. 6, emphasis added.
8 Ibid., par. 14.

[T]he ecclesial communities which have not preserved the
valid episcopate and the genuine and integral substance of
the eucharistic mystery, *are not churches in the proper sense*;
however, those who are baptized in these communities are
by baptism incorporated in Christ and thus are in a certain
communion, albeit imperfect, with the church. [9]

Before we get too worked up over this, let us remember that
historically, certain Protestant authors, including our esteemed
colleague John Calvin, did not hesitate to deny "true church" status
to Roman Catholicism. But that was a long time ago. The question
is, is such language appropriate today, after over thirty years of
fruitful ecumenical dialogue? Frankly, I associate this kind of
parochial language with fundamentalist churches and am dismayed
to find it still rearing its head in an official Catholic document.

In an article in the 28 October 2000 issue of *America* magazine, [10]
Francis A. Sullivan focuses on this section of the document, along
with the "Note on the Expression 'Sister Churches'" of 30 June
2000. The latter document sees this term as properly including only
"those ecclesial communities that have preserved a valid Episcopate
and Eucharist," [11] and thus excluding the Anglican and Protestant
churches, as noted in the letter by Dr. Nyomi.

Sullivan raises two questions: whether this narrow understanding
of the term "sister churches" is in fact consistent with Vatican II,
and whether thirty years of postconciliar dialogue calls for more
positive language about Anglican and Protestant communities.

Sullivan's argument revolves largely around Vatican II's expression
that the church of Christ *subsists in* the Catholic Church. Prior to the
council, official church documents identified the church "strictly

---

[9] Ibid., par. 17, emphasis added.
[10] Francis A. Sullivan, "The Impact of *Dominus Iesus* on Ecumenism: The
     strongest reactions have come from other Christian churches," *America* vol.
     183, no. 13 (28 October 2000): 8-11. I follow Sullivan closely in this section.
[11] Congregation for the Doctrine of the Faith, "Note on the Expression 'Sister
     Churches,'" published in *Origins*, vol. 30, no. 14 (14 September 2000), par. 12.

and exclusively" as the Catholic community of faith.[12] Vatican II's shift of language was intended to make a positive statement about Catholicism while softening the "negative implication" of the earlier position *vis-à-vis* other churches. However, when Leonardo Boff proposed that the church of Christ could be said to subsist also in other churches, he was roundly rebuffed in a 1985 *Notificatio* by the Congregation for the Doctrine of the Faith (C.D.F.)

Sullivan criticized this response by the C.D.F., arguing that

> the meaning of *subsistit* that best corresponds to its meaning in classical Latin, and to its context in the passage where it occurs, is "continues to exist." I further argued that in light of the "Decree on Ecumenism," one can conclude that the council meant to affirm that *the church Christ founded continues to exist in the Catholic Church with a fullness of the means of grace and of unity that are not found in any other church.* [13]

Sullivan notes that *Dominus Iesus* follows his interpretation of *subsistit* in paragraph 16, where it says:

> With the expression "subsistit in," the Second Vatican Council sought to harmonize two doctrinal statements: on the one hand, that the church of Christ, despite the divisions which exist among Christians, *continues to exist fully* only in the Catholic Church, and on the other hand, that "outside her structure, many elements can be found of sanctification and truth," that is, in those churches and ecclesial communities which are not yet in full communion with the Catholic Church.[14]

The key phrase, Sullivan insists, is "continues to exist fully." Only if this interpretation of *subsistit* is accepted can it be legitimately

---

12 Sullivan, "Impact of *Dominus Iesus*," 9.
13 Ibid., emphasis added.
14 *Dominus Iesus*, par. 16, emphasis added.

argued that the church of Christ subsists in no other church but the Catholic. [15]

Sullivan goes on to point out that *Dominus Iesus* does not say (as the C.D.F. earlier did in its response to Boff) that outside the visible structure of the Catholic Church there exist only "elements" of the church. Rather, it follows Vatican II in speaking of "Christian *communities* that are used by the Holy Spirit as means of salvation for their members." [16] It also follows Vatican II in referring to them as "ecclesial communities" rather than as "churches."

Having laid out this background, Sullivan proceeds to note three areas of difficulty with the document:

1. Vatican II "never flatly declared that the ecclesial communities are 'not churches in the proper sense,' as the C.D.F. has now done." He adds, "one would think that the progress made in more than thirty years of dialogue with those communities would have suggested a more positive recognition of their ecclesial reality." [17]

2. The Doctrinal Commission at Vatican II did make the following statement:

It must not be overlooked that the communities that have their origin in the separation that took place in the west are not merely a sum or collection of individual Christians, but they are constituted by social ecclesiastical elements which they have preserved from our common patrimony, and which confer on them a *truly ecclesial character*. In these communities *the one sole church of Christ is present*, albeit imperfectly, in a way that is somewhat like its presence in particular churches, and *by means of their ecclesiastical elements the church of Christ is in some way operative in them*. [18]

[15] Sullivan, "Impact of *Dominus Iesus*," 9.
[16] Ibid., 10, emphasis added.
[17] Ibid.
[18] Quoted in Sullivan, "Impact of *Dominus Iesus*," 10-11.

We might ask how one can reconcile the idea that "the church of Christ is in some way operative" in these "truly ecclesial" communities with *Dominus Iesus*'s claim that they are not really churches.

3. Pope John Paul II himself stated the following in his 1995 encyclical *Ut Unum Sit*:

> Indeed the elements of sanctification and truth present in the other Christian communities, in a degree which varies from one to the other, constitute the objective basis of the communion, albeit imperfect, which exists between them and the Catholic Church. To the extent that these elements are found in other Christian communities, *the one church of Christ is effectively present in them.* [19]

On the basis of these three points, we might suggest that *Dominus Iesus*'s denial that the Reformed communities are "churches in the proper sense" is out of line with the trajectory of contemporary church teaching on this matter, including that of the pope.

Sullivan concludes by suggesting that we need to balance the one-sided emphasis on validity of ministry (on the basis of which certain communities are deemed to be not properly churches) with an emphasis on the fruitfulness of this ministry. As he puts it, "There can be no doubt about the life of grace and salvation that has been communicated for centuries through the preaching of the word of God and other Christian ministry in the Anglican and Protestant churches." [20]

What disturbs me about *Dominus Iesus* is its tone of triumphalism and its apparent (even if not intended) belittling of other religious traditions, including Christian ones. One would think that we would be humbled by the mistakes we have made in the past in this regard—mistakes that our own pontiff has been publicly

---

[19] Pope John Paul II, *Ut Unum Sit* (1995), quoted in Sullivan, "Impact of *Dominus Iesus*," 11.

[20] Sullivan, "Impact of *Dominus Iesus*," 11.

acknowledging for the past several years. The following statement by Michael A. Fahey shows that I am not alone in my reaction:

> What many Catholics have been perceiving, and I believe quite justifiably, is that the Vatican is sending out mixed messages these days. While the pope is praying with non-Christians in Assisi, asking for forgiveness of the Jews at the Western Wall in Jerusalem, and admitting the sinfulness at least of members of the church (if not the church itself), the Congregation for the Doctrine of the Faith is speaking in terms that sound as triumphalistic as pre-Vatican II, or appealing to an ecclesiology closer to Pius XII's *Mystici Corporis* than to that of Vatican II's *Lumen Gentium*. [21]

Conclusion

Must *Dominus Iesus* be a stumbling block to Reformed-Catholic relations? I would say no, for three reasons:

1. Your church's response has already been most gracious and is cause for hope. I am grateful that you are still willing to talk to us, even though you may quite justifiably be offended by the arrogant and condescending tone of this document.
2. The position on "sister churches" held by the Congregation for the Doctrine of the Faith seems to be somewhat at odds with other official church statements, particularly those made by Vatican II and John Paul II.
3. Many Catholics are deeply committed to dialogue, and this document will not change that commitment. On the contrary, it will impel us to be more humble and sensitive in our conversations with other Christians.

Maybe this declaration has been a good development in one sense. It reminds us that we should not let ecumenical and interfaith

---

[21] Michael A. Fahey, "Am I My Sister's Keeper? The Vatican's New Letter on 'Sister Churches,'" *America* vol. 183, no. 13 (28 October 2000): 14.

dialogue turn into just a lot of nice talk, where real differences (about the church or anything else) are simply dismissed or trivialized. I personally have benefited greatly from my exposure to the Reformed tradition, and I want to continue to learn from it and be nourished by it. Indeed, it would be good for us to see all ecumenical and interfaith dialogue in this light: as an occasion for learning from one another. Is it any accident that the root of the word "disciple" means "to learn"?

7

Joint Declaration on Justification: Reformed Comments

Anna Case-Winters

Introduction

I begin my essay by noting three "remarkables."

First, on October 31, 1999, a truly remarkable step was taken in advancing the unity of the church. The Roman Catholic Church and the Evangelical Lutheran Church in America signed a *Joint Declaration on Justification*. Justification, you may recall, was a rather central and church-dividing issue at the time of the Reformation! It was at the heart of all the other disputes. How are we justified? What is the place of faith? What is the place of works? Now, to be able *today* to make a *joint* declaration on justification is a sign of how far things have come since then. Listen to one portion of what is mutually agreed—and listen with your Reformed antennae up!

> Together we confess: By grace alone, in faith in Christ's saving work and not because of any merit on our part, we are accepted by God and receive the Holy Spirit, who renews our hearts while equipping and calling us to good works (par. 15).[1]

1 *Joint Declaration on the Doctrine of Justification by the Lutheran World Federation and the Roman Catholic Church* (Grand Rapids: Eerdmans, 1999). The *Declaration*

Can you believe it? You may have to see it with your own eyes if you are as astonished upon first hearing as I was.

My second "remarkable" concerns the approach of the document. It is remarkably constructed to recognize both agreement and difference. Instead of endless debate to hammer out wording aimed at complete agreement and uniform expression, we have here what might be called a "differentiated consensus." The conclusion of the work on justification is that there *is* a consensus on basic understandings and that, although there remain differences in the explications, these are no longer the occasion for doctrinal condemnations. The anathemas of the sixteenth century do not apply to the contemporary partners (par. 13).

So each portion begins, "We confess together," and names the common ground. What follows are sections that might say, "Catholics have emphasized ...," or, "Lutherans have articulated this in this way...."

The third "remarkable" rests on us: now *we* have a remarkable opportunity. We of the Reformed family through the World Alliance of Reformed Churches (WARC) have been invited to respond to the declaration, perhaps even to add our own distinctive Reformed voice to what has been said here. I can envision us adding sections under each of the common affirmations, "and the Reformed have said it this way." It is an exciting prospect.

The World Alliance of Reformed Churches has begun to reflect upon how we may respond. In November of 2001, a delegation from the alliance met with theologians and church leaders from the Roman Catholic Church, the Lutheran World Federation, and the

is divided into major sections as follows: "Preamble," 1. "Biblical Message of Justification," 2. "The Doctrine of Justification as Ecumenical Problem," 3. "The Common Understanding of Justification," 4. "Explicating the Common Understanding of Justification," 5. "The Significance and Scope of the Consensus Reached." Section 4 is divided into seven subsections (4.1, 4.2, etc.) The document is also divided into paragraphs that are numbered in a single sequence. I shall make use of both kinds of notation (paragraph and section) to refer to the *Declaration* in the text of this essay.

World Methodist Council in a colloquium entitled, "The Joint Declaration on the Doctrine of Justification in a Wider Ecumenical Context." The participants agreed that a consultative process should be continued. The WARC delegation has proposed to the Executive Committee of WARC that we continue to explore whether and how we may express support for the agreements set forth in the *Joint Declaration on the Doctrine of Justification*. The question of what a Reformed voice might add has now become more than theoretical!

What will we say when they turn to us? Do we have anything distinctly our own to offer? Anything, that is, that cannot simply be subsumed under what the Lutherans have already said? I think we do have some things to add. The rest of my essay will review what is actually there in the joint declaration and begin to hint at what we might have to add that is both helpful and distinctive.

What Is There and What Might We Add?

The declaration begins with the consensus on defining justification—all in the direction of my introductory quotation. There is also common understanding that justification is not just any doctrine, but one that stands in essential relation to all others. Protestants have frequently insisted that it is the "article by which the church stands or falls" (*articulus stantis et cadentis ecclesiae*). It is the indispensable criterion that "serves to orient all the teaching and practice of our churches to Christ" (par. 18). After that consensus, which concludes section 3 of the document, some differentiation begins. Section 4, entitled "Explicating the Common Understanding of Justification," moves back and forth between agreement on essentials and difference in explication.[2]

---

2   In considering the discussion that follows, the reader may find a helpful resource in the articles "Justification," "Sanctification," and "Salvation," in *Encyclopedia of the Reformed Faith*, ed. Donald McKim (Louisville: Westminster/ John Knox, 1992).

4.1 "Human Powerlessness and Sin in Relation to Justification"

There is agreement regarding the powerlessness of human beings in relation to sin. "We confess together that all persons depend completely on the saving grace of God for their salvation" (par. 19). Both parties affirm dual and inseparable aspects to that grace: forgiveness of sins on the one hand and renewal of life on the other (par. 22).

4.2 "Justification as Forgiveness of Sins and Making Righteous"

But there is a difference regarding which is the primary effect of that saving grace. Lutherans have emphasized *forgiveness of sins*; we are only righteous in our union with Christ because he is our righteousness. Roman Catholics have insisted that forgiveness of sins brings with it a gift of new life which "in the Holy Spirit becomes effective in active love" (par. 24). Their emphasis is on *our being made righteous*.

Here is where we may have something distinctive to add: We have more equally balanced attention to forgiveness of sins with attention to renewal of life (sanctification). It might even be argued that Calvin is as much a theologian of sanctification as of justification.[3] He in fact held that these two together are a *duplex gratia*, a "twofold grace." Calvin assumed that our justification will have real effects in our lives, that we will be *regenerated*; and that faith will necessarily issue in good works. Yet neither our faith nor our works are our own—which would be a cause for boasting—but rather they are, equally, gifts of God. For Calvin—and maybe this could be a distinctive contribution—sanctification is not primarily about good works, but about "union with Christ." We do not attain or even approach sinless perfection, but "with a wonderful communion,

---

3 Gabriel Fackre, "The Joint Declaration and the Reformed Tradition," unpublished paper, 7.

day by day, he (Christ) grows more and more into one body with us, until he becomes completely one with us"[4] (Inst. 3.2.24).

Painting with broad strokes, the Roman Catholic view seems to give priority to sanctification while Lutheran theology seems to give priority to justification. I have found myself asking whether we are any closer to one of these than the other. Can it be that we have found the *via media* between these two positions? If so, that is a contribution we should share!

4.3 "Justification by Grace through Faith"

There is agreement that "faith is active in love and thus the Christian cannot and should not remain without works" and that "whatever in the justified precedes or follows the free gift of faith is neither the basis of justification nor merits it" (par. 25). As we have said, works are "the fruit and not the root" of our justification.

Lutherans have been concerned to underscore that this means it is "God that effects faith" (par. 26). It is nothing we do that opens the door or makes possible the giving of this gift, and there is nothing of our doing in opening our hand to receive it. Catholics want to add that justification and renewal are joined in Christ. With the caveat that the renewal of life "contributes nothing to justification about which one could boast," this is admitted (par. 27).

4.4 "The Justified as Sinner"

In the next section, there is agreement that "the justified must all through life constantly look to God's unconditional justifying grace. They also are continuously exposed to the power of sin still pressing its attacks and are not exempt from a lifelong struggle against the contradiction to God…" (par. 28).

But while the Lutherans press *simul iustus et peccator*, our being at the same time justified and a sinner, the Catholic view is that "the

---

[4]   John Calvin, *Institutes of the Christian Religion*, ed. John T. McNeill, trans. Ford L. Battles (Philadelphia: Westminster Press, 1960), 3.2.24.

grace of Christ imparted in baptism takes away all that is sin 'in the proper sense' and all that is 'worthy of damnation' (Rom. 8.1)" (par. 30). Here we have a differentiation that strains the consensus, I think, at two levels.

For the time being we have to bracket the first level, namely, our substantial differences in the sacramental theology as to what baptism "imparts." We do have our Reformed resistance to anything "automatic" here, the refusal of *ex opere operato*. We have sought to maintain the freedom of God and the necessity of faith for the full efficacy of the sacrament. We insist that the sign and the thing signified are to be connected but not identified. But bracketing that, for the time being, we zero in on differences around justification.

Gabriel Fackre has pointed out that there is a clear difference of understanding "how the saving work of Christ is applied—by imputation or impartation, by forensic declaration or by a 'quality intrinsically adhering to the soul.' And from this difference follows (*sic*) all the related divergences on concupiscence and the *simul*, merit and the place of works, law and gospel."[5] I think he is on to something here. This difference may well be the heart of all the other differences. At the very least they are all intertwined with one another.

Again I wonder, where are *we*? What happens when, as Fackre puts it, the Lutheran *simil* meets the Reformed *sanctificatio*?

We really do have a bit of a difference here. It is expressed in (among other places) Question 77 of the *Westminster Larger Catechism*: "Wherein do justification and sanctification differ? Although sanctification be inseparably joined with justification, yet they differ, in that God in justification imputeth the righteousness of Christ; in sanctification his Spirit infuseth grace and enableth to the exercise thereof; in the former sin is pardoned; in the other it is subdued...."[6]

5 Fackre, 7.
6 Presbyterian Church, (USA), *Book of Confessions* (Louisville: Office of the General Assembly, Presbyterian Church [USA]), 7.187.

While the Reformed accept the forensic character of justification—it is an event of God's grace—they refuse to separate this from sanctification as a process of growth in God's grace. As Question 35 of the *Westminster Shorter Catechism* puts it, "Sanctification is the work of God's free grace," and in it "we are enabled more and more to die unto sin and to live unto righteousness."[7] (Thus we are not only counted righteous but also made righteous, as justification and sanctification are grasped together.)

Here again we occupy a space between, and perhaps one that leans more toward the Roman Catholic view. It is not that there is no acknowledgement of sanctification in the Lutheran perspective, but it is so attenuated by the effort to avoid works righteousness that enthusiasm for it is severely chastened.

4.5 "Law and Gospel"

Moving ahead to the section on law and gospel, we have a somewhat similar situation. According to the consensus segment, "We confess together that persons are justified by faith in the gospel 'apart from works prescribed by the law' (Rom. 3:28). Christ has fulfilled the law and by his death and resurrection has overcome it as a way to salvation. We also confess that God's commandments retain their validity for the justified and that Christ has by his teaching and example expressed God's will which is a standard for the conduct of the justified also" (par. 31).

This seems well balanced enough to Reformed ears, until the Lutherans and Catholic offer their explications. We would disagree with both. The Lutherans comment that the theological use of the law is as "demand and accusation" (par. 32), so that in stating that it is still in effect they appear to mean that the law still demands and accuses. Here we would (predictably!) wish to add the Reformed conviction of a "third use of the law," the conviction of the positive guiding role of the law for the Christian life, the law as God's good

---

7   Ibid., 7.035.

gift to us. For us this is perhaps the most important aspect of its continuing validity.

The Catholic position is equally problematic, for while it also acknowledges a continuing validity of the law, this is presented as "God's commandments which the righteous are bound to observe." Here I think we would rather speak of the justified (rather than the righteous) being *set free* (rather than bound) to observe the law. The justified are set free to observe the law in lives of grateful and joyful response to God's grace.

So we would have "salutary admonitions" to offer to each here.

4.6 *"Assurance of Salvation"*

Under the topic of assurance of salvation, the declaration says, "We confess together that the faithful can rely on the mercy and promises of God. In spite of their own weakness and the manifold threats to their faith, on the strength of Christ's death and resurrection they can build on the effective promise of God's grace in Word and Sacrament and so be sure of this grace" (par. 34). There seem to be no significant differences between Lutheran and Roman Catholic perspectives on this topic.

If we were to add our voice it would probably not be to disagree but rather to ask what more needs to be said on this matter. Our doctrines of election and perseverance of the saints frame justification in divine sovereignty in a way that helpfully strengthens assurance of salvation and preempts the need for continual reassurance. A theocentric reframing of these affirmations has much to commend it.

What happens if we, as Gabriel Fackre has suggested, shift our focus from *sola fide* to *soli deo gloria*? This takes as our habit of thought a more theocentric than anthropocentric orientation. The objective dimensions of what God has done in Christ are given more attention than our subjective (and inevitably partial, wavering) appropriation of it. We are delivered out of much heavy contemplation of the state of our own souls. That is the case not only because God can be trusted but also because we realize that "it is not about us."

The issue calls to mind Calvin's response to Bishop Sadoleto when the bishop was warning that if Calvin cared about this own soul and the souls of his followers, he should return to the true church, so that they might get their sacraments from a reputable broker! Calvin responds with surprise that a religious man like the bishop should commend persons to be so concerned about the state of their own souls. As Calvin insists, our concern must be the glory of God. It is that to which we must attend.[8]

4.7 "The Good Works of the Justified"

On the good works of the justified, the declaration presents a balanced view in the consensus section: "We confess together that good works—a Christian life lived in faith hope, and love—follow from justification and are its fruits" (par. 37).

We are agreed. But the Catholics still want to talk about merit and how in the Bible a "reward in heaven is promised to these works," and they want to make clear that people are responsible for their actions (par. 38). The Lutherans do not want to talk in terms of merit and greatly diminish the importance of works.

It seems to me we stand with the Lutherans in refusing the whole category of merit. It raises a red flag of works righteousness. But certain considerations remain…

I cannot resist telling a story here. A fine elder from one of our Reformed churches died and presented herself at the pearly gates. Peter said, "I am sorry, but you are not to be admitted to heaven, you are going to have to go the other way." Perplexed, she did so, but when she got there she saw a face she recognized. "John Calvin! What are you doing here!" He pointed down the hall to another man and said, "Why don't you ask him. He started it." So she went over

---

8   John Calvin, "Reply to Sadoleto," trans. Henry Beveridge, in *A Reformation Debate*, ed. John C. Olin (New York: Harper Torchbooks, 1966), 58.

to the man. "Martin Luther! What are you doing here?" And he said very gruffly, "Works matter."

While we may want to reject the category of merit, we do well to reclaim insistence on responsibility of persons for their actions and the importance of works. We have always been as receptive to the book of James as to the book of Galatians. In the *Second Helvetic Confession*, the purpose of good works is laid out. They have nothing to do with "earning eternal life," rather they are "for the glory of God, to adorn our calling, to show gratitude to God, and for the profit of the neighbor."[9] Further on, the confession speaks in fairly strong language, "We therefore condemn all who despise good works and babble that they are useless and that we do not need to pay attention to them."[10] It seems we want to, at one and the same time, reject merit and affirm the importance of good works.

A strong social ethic and a world-engaged spirituality have grown out of Reformed sensibilities; these are rooted in our conviction regarding the sovereignty of God over all of life. This is a gift we have to offer, and we need to bring it to the table of ecumenical dialogue.

Conclusion

The *Joint Declaration on Justification* is truly a watershed. It must surely encourage anyone who cares about the unity of the church. Unity is of the essence of the church. It is a God-given reality. As the Reformed theologian Peter Hodgson has suggested, the very logic of Christian faith entails unity, for we are all oriented toward one single, solitary person and event—Jesus Christ. [11] Insofar as we are drawn to him, we are necessarily drawn to one another. The unity of the church is not something we can achieve—it is a gift of God. Nor is it something we can undo—it is a gift of God. Our divisions then, cannot destroy unity. Our concern is that divisions

---

9   *Book of Confessions*, 5.117.
10 Ibid, 5.119.
11 Peter Hodgson, *Revisioning the Church* (Philadelphia: Fortress Press, 1988).

obscure this unity, and they diminish our effectiveness and dilute our witness.

It is my hope that efforts like this one will multiply that our unity may become visible. That "we may be one...that the world may believe" (John 17:21). So when we are invited to the table of ecumenical dialogue, may the invitation find us ready with every good thing we have to offer.

8

A Reformed-Catholic Future: When Albany and Kigali Eclipse Geneva and Rome

Gregg A. Mast

Introduction

In a recent article entitled, "A Roman Catholic Vision of the Ecumenical Movement," Father John Ford writes:

> Every vision is influenced by memories of the past, conditioned by experiences in the present, and inspired by hopes for the future. In other words, every ecumenical vision is autobiographical. Accordingly, I would like to begin my presentation by sharing a few ecumenical reminiscences insofar as my personal memories are components of my own ecumenical vision and may serve as reminders of where American Roman Catholics have come from, as conditioning where we are at present on the wider ecumenical pilgrimage, and as possible prognosticators of where we might venture in the ecumenical future."[1]

I would like to follow in the footsteps of Father Ford and offer a brief word about, first, my own ecumenical journey; second, my

---

1   *Ecumenical Trends,* March 2001, 8.

growing realization that a Reformed-Roman Catholic future needs to begin again at the beginning, with our common baptism; and third, the evolving discovery that our future together will be greatly enhanced by participating in a challenging and revealing conversation with the Christian church in the southern hemisphere.

Past

First, a word about the past. I was born into a culture that divided the world into two parts—those who were Christian and those who were Catholic. Over the years, I have discovered that Catholics born and raised before Vatican II grew up in a similar universe. For me, the parochialism of this view of the world reached its apex when I entered Hope College and, in response to a question on a form asking me to indicate my religion, I wrote, "Reformed Church in America"—not Christian, not Protestant, not even Reformed, but Reformed Church in America.

My small world was deconstructed in a brief three-year period in the early 1970s by three events. First, I received a call to ministry in a high Lutheran Church in a South Philadelphia housing project, where Pastor Cochran celebrated a weekly Eucharist among hundreds of children. The cult of the church was a replacement for the cultic life of urban gangs. Second, while a student at New Brunswick Seminary, I served with the Roman Catholic ministry of Rutgers University. My spiritual compass was sent spinning as I received the Eucharist from the hands of Father Sebastian Muchelli. Third, the hands of that compass were steadied by the person and guidance of Howard Hageman who, long before, had come to see himself as both Catholic and Reformed.

It is in this section on the past that I would like to relate my experience as a participant in the Seventh Bi-Lateral Conversation between the Roman Catholic Church and three Reformed denominations. Over the past three years, representatives from the Presbyterian Church (USA), the United Church of Christ, and the Reformed Church in America have met regularly with a half dozen of our counterparts in the Roman Catholic Church in the United States. A Presbyterian pastor from Alabama and a bishop from northern Michigan cochaired the sessions.

I place this bi-lateral dialogue in the past because I am convinced that such conversations have produced as much as we can expect from them. The Roman Catholic Church has only been a participant in the ecumenical journey for the past thirty-five years, but its international character will continue to demand from the rest of us new ways to transcend both our denominational and national identities. Although our conversations were cordial and will lead to the joint publication of a resource for couples who seek marriage, there was no question that each tradition brought very limited authority, and thus limited vision, to the table. We could explain our theological positions found in liturgies, synodical and papal documents, and confessions, but we had neither the mandate nor the will to walk into new ecumenical territory.

The pastoral document, written by dialogue participants, has now been published.[2] It will be, I believe, a very helpful aid to congregational leaders and couples who are seeking to be married. It is eminently practical in its design, with case studies attached to each chapter. It addresses crucial questions, such as the marriage service itself, the sacramental issues around raising a family, and the ways in which a couple can remain committed to their respective traditions while serving as a common witness to both churches to which they belong.

The dialogue concluded that ecumenical families are a sign of judgment *and* a symbol of hope. They represent for all of us the painful limitations of two Christian traditions which cannot find their way to the same table to be nourished. At the same time, they represent for all of us a sign of how we can continue to live together in unity and learn from each other along the way. The covenant of

2 *Interchurch Families,* ed. John C. Bush and Patrick Cooney (Louisville: Geneva Press, 2002).

marriage into which a couple enters is both a reminder of our pain and a symbol of our hope.

When all was said and done, however, the Bi-Lateral Conversation chose to do little in moving us further along the ecumenical quest for oneness. It chose to do little because we had neither the authority nor the vision. Representatives from three national/ denominational bodies were in conversation with the national expression of a worldwide communion. Now, to be sure, greater understanding of each other's identities remains very helpful. We discovered again and again that, although we have lived as neighbors for thirty-five years, we often do not have a very clear sense of the beliefs and piety that inspire our faith. It would seem to me that the way forward in Bi-Lateral Conversations is to follow in the footsteps of the Lutherans in their remarkable agreement with the Vatican regarding justification, discussed by Anna Case-Winters in her essay in this volume. In the past year, the Presbyterian Church (USA) has also had two conversations with representatives of the Pontifical Council of the Promotion of Christian Unity. The Presbyterian Church graciously invited an observer from the Reformed Church in America to the first conversation, which happened in Louisville, Kentucky, in December, and the second at the Vatican, in March. The two traditions have included in their discussions the very difficult but crucial question of the papacy in response to the papal encyclical *Ut unum sint*, in which Pope John Paul II writes:

> I am convinced that I have a particular responsibility in this regard, above all in acknowledging the ecumenical aspirations of the majority of the Christian community, and in heeding the request made of me to find a new way of exercising the primacy which, while in no way renouncing what is essential to its mission, is nonetheless open to a new situation.[3]

3 *Encyclical Letter 'Ut unum sint'...on Commitment to Ecumenism* (Washington: United States Catholic Conference, 1995), par. 95.

Our Presbyterian sisters and brothers have responded that they would like to explore what may define the "new situation" to which His Holiness refers. While the Roman tradition brings to the table a great concern about the individual successor to Peter, it is clear that the Reformed tradition is far more interested in the successor to the Council of Jerusalem (Acts 15), which in turn holds the church faithful to apostolic faith and tradition.

It appears to me that our next steps toward a Roman Catholic/Reformed future are best pursued at a local level and an international one. With gratitude for thirty-five years of faithful national dialogue, I would humbly suggest that we turn for our present focus to the issue of baptism, and for our future vision to a common conversation with the dynamic church of the southern hemisphere. Pursuing this course will encourage us to discuss more clearly the gospel call in our twenty-first-century culture.

Present

I begin this section by directing our attention to the present challenge of a Reformed/Roman Catholic future. Let us consider first the words of St. Paul to the church in Corinth, when he echoes back to the struggling community the charges that have come to him:

> "…I belong to Paul," or "I belong to Apollos," or "I belong to Cephas," or "I belong to Christ." Has Christ been divided?… (1 Cor. 1:12-13).

Paul, missionary and pastor, carried on a love-hate relationship with the church he founded in Corinth. He was deeply loyal to this community of Christ, and at the same time he was regularly frustrated and perplexed by the divisions and disunity that troubled its life. Here in the first chapter of the first letter to the church in Corinth, Paul describes the factions that had developed in the community. Tragically, it appears that they were parties or loyalties that grew up around the persons by whom the members had been baptized. Already in the first century, we discover that the act of baptizing, a sacred washing so that the believer could become a member of the community of Christ, had given rise to divisions instead of unity. None of us need to go any further than the yellow pages in our local telephone directory in order to discover that the Corinthian crisis has not disappeared. The divisions of the Christian church are highlighted in bold point as denomination after denomination confronts the seeker. Has Christ been divided? The community that was called to be one was being torn apart.

The poetry of Paul's letter to the Ephesians, a letter that very well may have been a kind of circular letter to many of the first century churches, sings a different melody. "There is one body, and one Spirit, just as you were called to the one hope of your calling, one Lord, one faith, one baptism, one God and Father of all, who is above all and through all and in all" (Eph. 4:4-6).

We come to the issue of the catholicity of baptism with both tunes in our heads. How many of us claim first to be Presbyterian or Reformed or Lutheran? How many of us claim first to be Protestant, Roman Catholic, or Orthodox? *By* whom we were baptized has all too often taken precedence over *in* whom we were washed. The battles of the first century plague us still. And yet, in spite of all the echoes of the Corinthian church, it is the Ephesian hymn that remains not only our goal but also the foundation of our common life.

The liturgies of many churches have not forgotten the claim of sacramental oneness in Christ. Presbyterians welcome newly baptized members with these words, "John and Jane have been received into the one holy catholic and apostolic church through baptism."[4] The Reformed Church in America makes the following declaration: "In the name of the Lord Jesus Christ, the only King and Head of his Church, [Jane and John] are now received into the visible membership of the Holy Catholic Church...."[5] Other liturgies proclaim that the

---

4 *Book of Common Worship* (Louisville: Westminster/John Knox, 1993), 414.
5 *Order for Profession of Faith* (Reformed Church Press, 2001), 16.

baptized is received into the "household of God," or is a "member of the family of God," or is a "child of God, disciple of Christ, member of the church." Each of these phrases confronts the Corinthian crisis with an echo of the Ephesian confession.

The new catechism of the Roman Catholic Church states, "Baptism constitutes the foundation of communion among all Christians, including those who are not yet in full communion with the Catholic Church."[6] It would appear that although the foundation of Ephesians remains intact, the church has been built with lumber from Corinth. Christians are kept from the common meal of Christ as one tradition bars another. One baptism is not embraced by all parts of the church, as the Corinthians' cry, "Has Christ been divided?" continues to echo in our ears.

In spite of struggles, however, the gift and goal of unity remains. At our best moments, we yearn to gather around one table, we are washed with one baptism, and we reach out to serve a world of needs with common resources and commitment. The World Council of Churches' *Baptism, Eucharist, and Ministry* document calls us forward into such a new day:

> Churches are increasingly recognizing one another's baptism as the one baptism into Christ....Mutual recognition of baptism is acknowledged as an important sign and means of expressing the baptismal unity given in Christ. Wherever possible, mutual recognition should be expressed explicitly by the churches.[7]

In the encyclical, *Ut unum sint,* John Paul II exclaims that our unity is not to be found in "some large-hearted philanthropy or a vague spirit." Instead,

---

6 *Catechism of the Catholic Church* (Vatican City: Libreria Editrice Vaticana, 1997), 323.

7 *Baptism, Eucharist and Ministry.* Faith and Order Paper no. 111 (Geneva: World Council of Churches, 1982), par. B16.

it is rooted in recognition of the oneness of baptism and the subsequent duty to glorify God in his work. The Directory for the Application of Principles and Norms on Ecumenism expresses the hope that baptisms will be mutually and officially recognized. This is something much more than an act of ecumenical courtesy; it constitutes a basic ecclesiological statement.[8]

The *Directory for the Application of Principles and Norms on Ecumenism* furthers this agenda by stating that this quest for baptismal unity needs to be accomplished at a local level:

It is strongly recommended that the dialogue concerning both the significance and the valid celebration of baptism take place between Catholic authorities and those of other church and ecclesial communities at the diocesan or Episcopal conference levels.[9]

Building on this encouragement, the Roman Catholic Diocese of Albany, New York, and the local Capital Area Council of Churches initiated six years ago a unique program, entitled, Ecumenical Witnesses at Baptism. More than a dozen different denominations and almost fifty witnesses have participated in the program. Quite simply, a congregation that is about to baptize invites the coordinator of the program to send baptismal witnesses from other traditions. Their liturgical participation is determined by the inviting congregation, but often they are encouraged to stand and verbally affirm the baptism as a rite of entrance into the church catholic. Their presence is a powerful and poignant sign of the church opening her arms and receiving the baptized into a worldwide communion that transcends boundaries of nations, space, and time.

8 *Ut unum sint*, par. 42.
9 (Vatican City: Secretariat for Christian Unity, 1993), par. 94.

But as dramatic as such a local program is, it remains stymied by the canon law of the Roman church and the varying customs of other participating denominations. For the one baptized is not only received into the church catholic, a statement most Christians affirm, but also into a local expression of that church, or, for our brothers and sisters in the Roman church, into the Roman Catholic Church. This statement again highlights the continuing struggle to define rites of initiation, baptism, first communion, and confirmation. The *Directory for the Application of Principles and Norms on Ecumenism* clearly identifies the nagging problem:

> Every Christian has the right for conscientious religious reasons, freely to decide to come into full Catholic communion. The work of preparing the reception of an individual who wishes to be received into full communion with the Catholic Church is of its nature distinct from ecumenical activity. The Rite of Christian Instruction of Adults provides a formula for receiving such persons into full Catholic communion.[10]

As a Reformed pastor and theologian, I cannot help but smile when I hear the phrase, "full communion." It is a concept with which we struggled mightily when discussing the right of children to be present at the Lord's Table.[11] Now we hear it again as we try to envision a way for the one who is baptized with water into the Triune God not only to be received by all of us, but by each of us. How is it possible to acknowledge the baptism of a person into the universal church without acknowledging at the same time that they are members of a church, not an ecclesial community? Indeed, how is it possible to affirm a common baptism and not be inspired to exclaim that the family is called to eat together at one table?

It is here that our pastoral and sacramental theologians and canon lawyers need to come together in service of the church. It would

---

10 Ibid., par. 99.
11 See *Minutes of the General Synod of the RCA,* 1988, 380-86.

seem to me that the most difficult part of the puzzle has already been solved with the acknowledgement of a common baptism. With His Holiness, Pope John Paul II, let us look to local expressions of the church to hammer out agreements that will allow us to live together in a sacramental and spiritual communion. Let Geneva and Rome be eclipsed by Albany and New Brunswick, and Paris and Nairobi. Geneva and Rome will finally seek to follow those who get their hands wet in the font and their feet dirty in the mud of ministry, as the heads of the baptized glisten with grace and hope for a new day.

Pope John Paul II, in a homily delivered to an Ecumenical Celebration of the Word in the Roman Basilica of St. Paul-Outside-the-Walls at the close of the Week of Prayer for Christian Unity in January, 2001, told delegates from twenty-three churches and ecclesial communities,

> The dialogues which have developed since the Second Vatican Council have brought a new awareness of the heritage and task common to Christians, and have produced very significant results. We have not yet of course reached the goal, but we have taken important steps forward. From being far apart and, often adversaries—as we once were— we have grown closer and our baptism incorporates us into one Body of Christ, in a communion that, while not yet full, is nonetheless real (cf. *Ut unum sint,* pars. 41-42). We have every reason to praise the Lord and thank him.[12]

Future

We open our eyes and hearts now to a Reformed-Roman Catholic future by turning toward the church which has taken root in the

---

[12] The English text of the homily is apparently currently available only on the Internet, at <http://www.vatican.va/holy_father/john_paul_ii/homilies/2001/documents/hf_jp-ii_hom_20010125_christian-unity_en.html>

rich, fertile, spiritual soil of Africa, Asia, and South America. Allow me to begin with a story.

A year and a half ago, I was invited by the World Alliance of Reformed Churches (WARC) to participate in a new dialogue with the "indigenous" or "instituted" churches of Africa. About a dozen pastoral theologians and leaders were gathered from both WARC and the indigenous African churches for an initial gathering in Kigali, Rwanda. Of those who gathered around the table on a Thursday morning in October 2000, I was the only non-African. What a tremendous privilege it was to be invited to such a family reunion. The indigenous churches in Africa, representing more than fifty million Christians on that continent, are in many cases communions which were formed out of the missionary churches that shared the gospel in Africa. The oldest indigenous churches are eighty or ninety years old and emphasize the expression of the gospel in terms of authentic African worship, piety, and leadership.

The first dialogue in Kigali spent considerable time struggling with the issue of polygamy. A few years ago, the World Council of Churches voted to deny membership to an indigenous African church that tolerated polygamy among those who had already practiced it before coming to the faith. The vote was viewed as a stinging rebuke of these African churches, which embrace with one arm the gospel and with the other the African culture. For me, indigenous African churches have the feeling of first-century Christianity as they affirm a world divided between good and evil spirits and the call of the church to be a healer not only of the body but also of the spirit. Tribal expectations, which often are deeply spiritual and animistic, challenge these African churches to affirm the African spirit with the Christian gospel. Of particular concern is the challenge urbanization poses to village leadership models. This challenge at times has meant that "charismatic chiefs" have been allowed to exercise their considerable authority unwisely and to the detriment of the faith.

The second gathering of the dialogue took place in Lagos, Nigeria, on the first weekend of March 2001. At this gathering, we struggled with the role of the Holy Spirit in the life of the church. When all was said and done, we affirmed together the necessity to judge the identity of a spirit against the revelation of scripture and within the context of a praying and thus discerning community of faith.

I tell this story to suggest that my brief interchanges in Africa, as well as my travel over the years among churches in Central America, Cuba, the Middle East, and India, confirm for me that distinguishing the gospel from culture, or discovering the identity of the gospel in culture, is a gift that can be enhanced dramatically through our conversations with Christians in the South. There is little doubt that the center of the Christian faith is shifting from Geneva, Rome, New York, and Moscow, to Kigali, Johannesburg, Sao Paolo, and Seoul. As we, meaning both the Roman Catholic and Reformed traditions, continue to disentangle ourselves from the culture in which we have strived and in which our witness is in many ways declining, we can benefit greatly from a *common* dialogue with our newest Christian sisters and brothers.

For some of us, this dialogue will be difficult initially, for in societies and churches that are striving to define themselves, the Christian faith is often painted in austere colors. We, the people of the West and the North, bristle at what we perceive to be the somewhat legalistic, parochial stance of the church of the Southern Hemisphere. There is nothing inherently "progressive" about being a citizen of the South—an observation that comes as a jolt to the liberals among us. But if we are to be led into a new millennium of service and proclamation, voices that do not carry the accents of Tübingen and Harvard, Rome and Geneva, need to be heard and heeded.

If the church catholic is going to be truly a world church in the age to come, it needs to hear the voice of those to whom we were sent, and the voice of those who now come to us with the gospel. North

America and Europe are the mission fields which will benefit most from those who have struggled to transcend the Reformation struggles in order to help us evangelize a culture which is quickly losing its soul. The future of Reformed-Roman Catholic relations will be defined more clearly as both our traditions sit quietly and alertly with those who will bring new eyes and hearts to our conversations. The struggle of the enculturation of the gospel, one faced by both of our traditions, will benefit by a common presence at the same tables of conversation in the South. Indeed, for once we will be sitting on the same side of the table. Our vision for a new world means that Geneva and Rome will be eclipsed by the conversations and insights which will take place in Kigali and Lagos, in Nairobi and Johannesburg, in Sao Paolo and Seoul and Jakarta.

Conclusion

The story is told that at the beginning of the Jubilee Year, the pope invited the archbishop of Canterbury, George Carey, and the representative of the ecumenical patriarch to accompany him to the massive doors of St. Peter's. They were to be opened for the year of the Jubilee, but the pope, frail with age, or perhaps wise in his responsibilities, could not budge the doors by himself. Rather, it required the work of all three leaders to move the doors. Alone it is difficult, indeed impossible, to make a difference. Together we are allowed to open the doors that lead to the fulfillment of Christ's prayer for unity.

Walter Kasper, the newly elected president of the Council for Promoting Christian Unity and recently appointed cardinal, has observed that "the ultimate ecumenical aim is not a uniform united church, but one church in reconciled diversity."[13] The phrase, "a church in reconciled diversity," is one borrowed from various

---

[13] Quoted in Robert Leicht, "Cardinals in Conflict," *The Tablet,* 28 April 2001, 608.

European Reformed churches. We will need to return to a clear focus on *in whom* we are baptized, rather than *by whom* the water was poured. And we will need to understand that if the gospel is to be allowed to be good news for the whole world, it will need to find its new face and soul with honest dialogue with those who live and pray in the Southern Hemisphere.

A prayer for unity challenges us to be one "so that the world will believe" (John 17:21). It is a prayer first uttered on the night of Jesus' betrayal in the shadow of the cross. It is a prayer we have ignored at the expense of the world. The future we seek is not for ourselves but for the world God loves. We need to feel again the common water of our baptism glisten with grace and hope. We need to come to the table not because we are filled with faith, but because we are hungry for it—not because we are whole, but because we are broken and seek the wholeness only Christ can offer. And in the future, the mahogany and stone tables and altars of Rome and Geneva will be slowly moved aside so there will be room for the intimate, common tables of Albany and Kigali where I pray we will finally sit together to be fed.

9

Reformed and Evangelical:
New Questions and Old

Allan Janssen

When the General Synod voted to submit an application for membership in the National Association of Evangelicals (NAE)—an application which is still pending as the present volume goes to press—the Reformed Church embarked upon a new venture in the expression of its ecumenical commitment. Because this venture is new, the Reformed Church is confronted with a number of novel questions. At the same time, the questions are old; it will be the burden of this essay to show just how the Reformed Church has lived with these questions in various guises. Further, I hope to support the claim that the questions raise a number of issues of Reformed identity, thus making our inquiry appropriate for the inauguration of a center for Reformed Church studies.

I will ask three short questions: First, *who*? With whom are we engaging in our application to join the NAE? Second, *how*? How do we engage in ecumenical encounter? And third, *why*? What is the purpose, or goal, of approaching the evangelical community in this way? What is the intended outcome?

Who?

First then, who? I am not asking the often-mooted question, just what is an "evangelical"? For our purposes, we will accept the NAE's definition in its "statement of principles" that stands as prologue to its constitution. It will become evident that the question of evangelical identity is important when we encounter the assertion of the Reformed Church that it is evangelical. For the present, I bracket that question out.

Instead, I frame the question from within our ecumenical commitment. When the church is about ecumenicity, it engages another *church* or *churches*. Equivalence exists between the partners in conversation—one church to another. This equivalence is articulated in the first sentence of the "Preamble" to the *Book of Church Order*: "The purpose of the Reformed Church in America, *together with all other churches of Christ,* is to minister...."[1] At the outset, the Reformed Church states that it is not the sole church but in fact ministers with other churches. But it does so as it engages other ecclesial communions in conversation. Those discussions are usually rigorous and challenging to the commitments of all communions involved. My point is that when the church makes or responds to ecumenical initiatives, it does so with parallel bodies, that is, with other churches, not with individuals or associations. When the Reformed Church enters the councils of churches, it does not enter into a relation with a council, or not primarily so, but through the various councils it engages other churches.

The question as we apply for membership with the NAE, then, is: with whom are we entering relation? Is it with an "association?" Is it with evangelical churches? Or is it with other believers? The last question presents itself because the NAE is an association of evangelicals—plural. Its name hints that this is an association that includes individuals. Indeed, its constitution allows not only what we might call parachurch organizations to be members, but

---

1   *The Book of Church Order* (New York: Reformed Church Press 2000), 1.

individuals as well. That is fine and well for the NAE. I am simply posing the question for ourselves: with whom are we talking?

Here I might comment that by asking this question I am raising the issue of ecclesiology. If the church is in some way central to the Reformed commitment, and I think that assumption can be substantiated easily by a quick look at the church's confessional basis, then we need to ask ourselves just how the church *as* church lives and acts with groups of Christians as individuals or in association who do not understand themselves as church.[2]

But perhaps the identity of the "who" is in fact not really the NAE, evangelical churches, or an amorphous body of evangelicals who, some in the media are telling us, are overrunning the contemporary religious landscape. I suggest that the "who" may well be those within our own communion who either identify themselves as evangelical or insist that the Reformed Church in America (RCA) is itself evangelical within their understanding of the term.

And that, I want to argue, is a very old question indeed within the Reformed communion. Here I shall make a rather long historical note. Within that branch of the Reformed from whence the RCA emerges, I reach back to that era within the Dutch Reformation denoted by the term *nadere reformatie*—the "further Reformation." In about the last half of the seventeenth century, a century after the Reformation had taken hold in the lowlands, the "further Reformation" emerged as a movement within the Reformed church. It was a reaction to formal orthodoxy and to a sterile commitment to doctrine. It demanded that the Reformation of the church alone was not sufficient but needed to continue as a reformation of the inner and ethical life of the individual believer. It went *further*. It was signaled early on by the brothers Johannes and Maximiliaan Teelinck, preachers from Zeeland. Their writings, under the influence of

---

2 The importance of the church as a theological reality is indicated by the fact that the Belgic Confession dedicates nine of its thirty-seven articles to the church.

English Puritans, influenced many with their zeal for a mystical, experiential religion that gave priority to inner piety above the purity of doctrine.[3] Their influence produced within the Dutch Reformed tradition a particular stream, including such persons as Voetius, van Lodenstein, and Koelman.

The Dutch historian Otto de Jong comments that the *nadere reformatie* was later to "narrow" to pietism. That pietism would desire "individual experience of communion with God, sanctification attuned to personal practices of piety."[4]

What makes this venture into old Dutch Reformed history relevant is the fact that this stream of pietism found its way to American shores in the eighteenth century. Randall Balmer has argued persuasively that American evangelicalism has its roots not only in New England Puritanism but also in the Dutch pietism of the middle colonies. This pietism too was a revolt against formality, ceremonialism, scholasticism, and moral laxity. It emphasized spiritual discipline and affective religion. It would insist on the necessity of spiritual rebirth.[5] And as the members of the *coetus* were the winners of that dust-up and thus made possible the establishment of the Reformed Church as an independent body in this country, the influence of Dutch pietism was to have a profound influence on what would become the Reformed Church in America. Students of Reformed Church history will know that Dutch pietists were to be found largely in the later *coetus* of the famous *coetus-conferetie* dispute.[6] The question of evangelical identity within the Reformed Church stands, then, at the outset of the American church's history.

3   J. Reitsma, *Geschiedenis van de Hervorming en de Hervormde Kerk der Nederlanden*, 4th ed. (Utrecht: Kemink & Zoon, n.d.), 374, 375.

4   Otto de Jong, *Nederlandse Kerkgeschiedenis* (Nijkerk: G.F. Callenbach, 1978), 236, translation mine.

5   Randall Balmer, *Blessed Assurance: A History of Evangelicalism in America* (Boston: Beacon Press, 1999), 16, 17.

6   A full account of the *coetus-conferetie* matter can be found in Gerald F. De Jong, *The Dutch Reformed Church in the American Colonies* (Grand Rapids: Eerdmans, 1978), 178 ff.

Balmer makes the point that Dutch pietism of the eighteenth century occurred within the ambit of the First Great Awakening, and thus had a decided Calvinist bent. By the beginning of the nineteenth century, with the "new measures" of the Second Great Awakening, revival took an Arminian turn. That was to put pressure on those Reformed who tended in the direction of "experimental," or what we would call experiential, religion. In part the Reformed found their way into the evangelical culture of the nineteenth century. I have pointed out elsewhere that the professor of practical theology at New Brunswick, James Cannon, accepted evangelicalism of a "modest sort" to which he gave "qualified approval." His lectures would caution future pastors against the overheated emotionalism of extreme exemplars of the new measures, and he would warn against high expectations of "general awakenings."[7]

The pressure brought by the evangelical/Arminian movement, however, resulted in schism. The dispute that led to the formation of the True Dutch Reformed Church arose in part in response to the frontier situation where conversions and awakenings could take place. (The frontier situation was neither the only, nor perhaps even the presenting issue. The orthodox were as concerned about Hopkinsian "liberalism.") At issue was the Dortian article on limited atonement, the assertion that Christ died for the particular number of elect. The more orthodox party wanted to hold the line. When the General Synod was forced to decide on the issue, it fudged. It wanted to be able to join the evangelical empire while at the same time to hold to its confessional background.[8] One can see an evangelical-orthodox divide within the Reformed Church itself.

---

7   See Allan Janssen, *Gathered at Albany*, Historical Series of the Reformed Church in America, no. 25 (Grand Rapids: Eerdmans, 1995), 40.

8   James Van Hoeven, "Dort and Albany: Reformed Theology Engages ad New Culture," in idem, ed., *Word and World: Reformed Theology in America*, Historical Series of the Reformed Church in America, no. 16 (Grand Rapids: Eerdmans, 1986), 18-22.

I add one final note to press the point. When, by the mid-nineteenth century, descendants of that stream in the Netherlands that found its source in the *nadere reformatie* began to come to this country in protest against the degeneration of the old Reformed faith, they found a congenial welcome (or congenial enough for a goodly number to find and remain within the Dutch church in America). Elton Eenigenburg claims that both the American church and the immigrants were deeply influenced by Voetian piety. He writes, "The warm evangelical piety of the immigrants was more than likely similar to that espoused by the already existing Protestant Dutch Church in North America."[9]

By now, I trust, my point is sufficiently clear. When we think of "evangelicals" we are not only thinking of Christians outside the Reformed Church who would describe their faith in terms of experiential piety with its emphasis on personal probity and spiritual rebirth. The "who" question then modulates to ask: who are we? Perhaps more pointedly, it also asks whether we are using our approach to the NAE as a substitute for holding the sort of conversation we should be having with ourselves.

How?

The second question that our approach to the NAE sets before us is the "how" question. How do we go about ecumenical conversation? Or, put another way, what are the ground rules? The Reformed Church has functioned ecumenically with a particular understanding. This can be illustrated by examining the ground rules for participation in the World Council of Churches (WCC). Membership in that council is open to churches that agree with the "basis" on which the council is founded, namely, that the WCC is a "fellowship of churches which confess the Lord Jesus Christ as God and Savior according to the scriptures and therefore seek to fulfill together their common calling to the glory of one God,

---

[9] "New York and Holland," in Van Hoeven, 43.

Father, Son and Holy Spirit."[10] That statement commits the Reformed Church to a certain position, viz., christocentric, scriptural, and trinitarian. But it clearly does so within the ambit of the ecumenical creeds that the Reformed join in confessing. Any number of crucial matters of doctrine, liturgy, and order are not mentioned in the WCC "basis."

In fact, membership in a council of churches enables the church to engage in both dialogue and common mission with churches whose commitments in matters of doctrine, liturgy, and order are quite different from our own, or even, from our perspective, wrong. Such matters indeed become the substance of discussion. The council is a place where divisive issues can be explicitly placed on the table. The Reformed Church does not enter the ecumenical world with only those churches with which it agrees. What would be the point? Were the churches to agree, the issue would be: what possible reason can the churches give to remain separated as church?

The "how" question has a new place because the Reformed presence in the NAE commits us to a new set of ground rules. The Constitution of the NAE includes a "Statement of Faith" (Article III) consisting of seven points. Its constitution goes on to say that "membership shall require adherence without reservation to the Statement of Faith" (Article IV).[11] Two assertions in that statement may serve to suggest both the nature of "adherence" and the reason why this requirement presents the Reformed Church with new ground rules. The first assertion is, "We believe the Bible to be the inspired, the only infallible, authoritative Word of God" (III.1). The second is, "We believe in the deity of our Lord Jesus Christ, in his virgin birth, in his sinless life, in his miracles, in his vicarious and atoning death through his shed blood, in his bodily resurrection, in

---

10 "World Council of Churches Constitution," www.wcc.coe.org/wcc/who/con-e.html.

11 "Constitution and By-laws," www.nae.net/about-constitution.html.

his ascension to the right hand of the Father, and in his personal return in power and glory" (III.3).

Two matters are at hand here. In contradistinction from what a church assents to in becoming part of, say, the WCC, the statement of faith of the NAE displays a considerable narrowing. A church is obliged to make considerably more defined doctrinal commitments on a number of matters judged essential by the association. I do not maintain that the association cannot or should not set such requirements as a condition for membership. I am only emphasizing that for the *Reformed* to consider uniting with a group with that sort of statement of faith is to play by a new set of rules, for in the ecumenical "game," such statements would themselves become items of conversation. The conversation may be intense and sometimes uncomfortable, and indeed one church or another may claim some such statement as a confession of faith and, as such, essential to the existence of the church. The "how" of our ecumenical conversation is at issue.

The second matter goes the heart of Reformed identity. The Reformed Church is to a large extent *constituted* by its confessional documents (in addition to its liturgy and its church order[12]). To signal an adherence "without reservation" to the statement of faith of the NAE, or any statement of faith for that matter, is to make a new confessional claim for itself. That claim in turn raises two issues for the Reformed Church, material and formal.

The formal issue has to do with making any confessional claim at all. Confession is a serious matter, one that would involve the entire church. (Interestingly and oddly, the Reformed Church has no mechanism for issuing a new confession[13]). But that is an odd, and

---

[12] See Daniel J. Meeter, *Meeting Together in Doctrine, Liturgy, & Government*, Historical Series of the Reformed Church in America, no. 24 (Grand Rapids: Eerdmans, 1993).

[13] See Allan Janssen, *Constitutional Theology: Notes on the Book of Church Order of the Reformed Church in America*, Historical Series of the Reformed Church in America, no. 33 (Grand Rapids: Eerdmans, 2000), 260.

at the very least new, situation. *Before* it embarks on this particular ecumenical venture the church must adjust itself to its new ecumenical partners. It is, as it were, to begin at the end, to have to come to agreement before a church enters ecumenical engagement. This is so whether or not the Reformed Church could in fact adhere to a proposed statement of faith. After all, the doctrinal formulations are indeed *formulations* and as such their syntax, grammar, etc., are crucially important.

That is so at the formal level alone. But the material issue also raises questions. Take the two statements at issue. The claim of the Bible to be the only infallible, authoritative Word of God leads the Reformed Church beyond its own confessional statements. The one place where the Reformed confessions articulate an understanding of the Word, articles 2-7 of the Confession of Faith (commonly called the "Belgic Confession"), is very artfully and carefully drawn. There we read, for example, that God "commanded his servants the Prophets and Apostles to commit his revealed Word to writing" (Article 2). Note that the confession can then speak of the Bible as the Word, but it is so secondarily. The "revealed" Word had been spoken by humans, then to be committed to writing. But then the Bible itself is not the only infallible, authoritative Word of God. To agree to such a claim would at the very least be a new clarification and, I would argue, a narrowing of the Reformed Church's current confessional commitment.[14]

Or take the other statement already adduced, that one must believe in the deity of Christ. Given the ecumenical creeds, the Reformed would gladly agree. Here, though, the formulation comes into play. For if we assert the deity apart from the humanity,

---

14 This point is made clearly in the Second Helvetic Confession, chapter 1, where it is confessed that the "preaching of the Word of God is the Word of God." *The Constitution of the United Presbyterian Church in the United States of America, Part I, Book of Confessions* (Philadelphia: The Office of the General Assembly, 1966), 5.004. This essay, of course, limits itself to the confessional statements in the Constitution of the RCA.

we have then betrayed the ecumenical creeds. One can, of course, appreciate the NAE's desire and need to affirm the deity of Christ against assaults on that doctrine; confessions are often of their very nature polemical. Still, one would expect the church (as church, we might add, and not as a movement within the church) to spend considerable time and effort articulating its faith in a more nuanced manner.

Thus the "how" question has to do with whether the church must first attain unity of doctrine before it can enter ecumenical relations. In the modern ecumenical movement the Reformed, along with other churches, proceed knowing that such doctrinal differences are vitally important, but they do not expect to work them out prior to ecumenical engagement, nor do they think it necessary to work them out in order to acknowledge another church as church. That is what is new. Still, the question has been around for a long while within the Reformed family. Is the unity of the church to be found in confessional agreement? After all, the Reformed call their confessions "Standards of Unity"; adherence to the confessions is what holds the churches together. Early synods of the Dutch Reformed church would each begin by claiming afresh the doctrinal standards. But is that where unity in fact is to be found? Or is the unity of the church to be found extrinsically, outside itself?

A theologian within the tradition, J.H. Gunning, Jr., articulated the issue clearly. Gunning, a theologian in the Netherlands Reformed Church in the late nineteenth century, spoke to a church actively struggling with confessional issues. He wrote at the time when Abraham Kuyper was at the height of his influence and the Gereformeerden presented an alternate approach to confessional commitments.[15] Gunning had a deep yearning for the unity of the church. In a letter to his friend Martin Kahler, he wrote that although the division within the church may be historically necessary,

---

[15] For an account in English of these developments in the Netherlands, see James Bratt, *Dutch Calvinism in Modern America* (Grand Rapids: Eerdmans, 1984), 3-33.

"it presents itself to me as being against the Lord's will. The unity of John 17:21 is not only something desirable, but something absolutely necessary."[16] He believed that the Gereformeereden, as separatists, took a wrong approach. He could sympathize, for he maintained that the approach of the main church was also wrong-headed. Unity could not be had at the expense of the holiness of the church, and a broad tolerance that allowed unchecked plurality of doctrine led to the degeneration of the church.

He put the question in terms of the great attributes of the church as articulated in the Nicene Creed. Given that the church must be both holy and catholic, the question was: from which end do you begin? With catholicity or with holiness?[17] He argued that the church could not begin with holiness, as did the Gereformeerden, for to do so would be to lose the catholicity of the church. Furthermore by so doing, only the holy ones, only those who express agreement with the confession, i.e., the particular confessional writings, can be part of the church. This located unity in the articulated faith of individual believers, or in collections of believers—a notion of unity that could work for parties within the church, but not for the church as church. What of those of other times and places who articulate the faith differently? He claimed that a unity formed around confessional writings is only a "surrogate" for unity.[18]

Gunning argued that the church must begin from unity, and not just from pragmatic considerations. Rather, the church begins from unity because the church *is* one, and its unity is not located within itself, its confession, its order, or its liturgy. Unity is not ours but comes from Christ. Gunning does not see this unity as static, as though the church's unity subsists in Christ as an already

---

16 Cited in E.J. Beker and M.G.L. den Boer, *J.H.Gunning, Jr. Een theologisch portret* (Baarn: Ten Hoeve, 1979), 22, translation mine.

17 W. Balke, "Hoedemaker, Gunning, Kraemer en van Ruler," in W. van 't Spijker, et. al., *De Kerk: Wezen, weg en werk van de kerk naar reformatorische opvatting* (Kampen: De Groot Goudriaan, n.d.), 211 ff.

18 Balke, *De Kerk*, 218.

accomplished reality. While that may be so from one perspective, Gunning has a more eschatological understanding. "The Lord our Savior alone can and will give it [unity]."[19] Furthermore, this unity is trinitarian as it is the indwelling of the Spirit that brings unity.

On the one hand, the Reformed Church appears to have chosen the route outlined by Gunning. The *Ecumenical Mandate* adopted by the General Synod of 1996[20] claims as the first foundation of Christian unity that unity is "derived from the spiritual fellowship of the Father and the Son and is a work of the Holy Spirit." Unity is an article of faith. The mandate goes on to claim that Christian unity is "already and not yet." "...[E]cumenical ministry must be carried on eschatologically...." The foundations conclude with the claim that Christian unity is "unity in truth." The mandate warns against the danger of making "an idol of unity at the expense of doctrine." Confessional unity is not lost, then, but is clearly subsidiary to the eschatological union already the church's in Christ through the Spirit.

On the other hand, part of what lurks behind the hesitance among some toward the Reformed Church's participation in the *Formula of Agreement* is the suspicion that a partner church does not practice the "pure preaching of the gospel," one of the marks of the true church articulated in the confession of faith. And since the church's only way of judging the "pure preaching" is against the measure of the confessions, we would need to come to confessional agreement. This has been made more problematic as certain matters of conduct or personal probity are being touted as of confessional status. I do not intend to belittle the issue; the place and status of confession are crucially important to the Reformed Church, and it a matter about which there exist differing understandings. I have only intended to show that the Reformed Church's application to join the NAE surfaces questions that have been around in the Reformed churches for a good while. They are not only new, but also old.

---

[19] Balke, *De Kerk*, 217.
[20] *Minutes of the General Synod, RCA*, 1996, 197 (approval); 1995, 174-186 (text).

Why?

The third question is "why?" Why does the Reformed Church desire membership in the NAE? How does that action further the Reformed Church's ecumenical commitment? The approach to the NAE sets the question in a new context. Given the nature of the NAE (and I repeat, it is not my intention to question the integral nature of the NAE), surely the goal would not be to promote structural unity of the churches. Neither would it be conciliar; the Reformed Church is not entering a communion of communions. Again, it would not be to engage in dialogue over essential matters that have divided the churches; the NAE has its statement of faith, and those who signal their adherence are free to unite. That is not dialogue, nor does it pretend to be.

So why? In its report to the General Synod recommending application to the NAE, the Commission on Christian Unity gave as reasons that the application completes conversations under way and that to submit the application would honor the urging of the various assemblies of the church—hardly ecumenical reasons. Then the commission added that membership in the NAE supports the claim in the *Ecumenical Mandate* that the Reformed Church is both ecumenical and evangelical.[21] That statement raises, of course, the question of just what it means to be "evangelical." And I am compelled to ask if that means that the Reformed Church understands "evangelical" in the manner articulated in the NAE's statement of faith. If so, as I argued above, we have a great deal of work to do, for it is far from clear that the Reformed Church so understands itself. At the very least, it has never so claimed or confessed.

A closer look at the *Ecumenical Mandate* will disclose that the answer to our "why" question is ambiguous at best. There, under "criteria for establishing and maintaining ecumenical relations," we find that the Reformed Church will "give particular attention to

---

21 *Minutes of the General Synod, RCA*, 2000, 103-104.

building ecumenical bridges of fellowship and partnership between conciliar bodies and 'evangelical' churches and agencies, in order to enhance the healing of our divisions for the sake of our common witness." It appears, then, that it is "common witness" that is the goal.[22]

Fair enough. In fact, the criteria emerge from the goals as articulated in the mandate. There one does *not* find, for example, church union as a goal. Instead, the church will move into "greater expressions of unity with those endeavors which seek to model and promote Christian unity in the world." One also finds as a goal that the Reformed Church will move toward "embracing full communion with other churches...." These goals manifest that the Reformed Church does not seek church union as a goal but is struggling to find a goal and reason for its ecumenical work. That, of course, is not unique to the Reformed Church as the churches enter a new generation of ecumenicity. It fairly describes the state of the ecumenical movement at present.

But I wonder. Is there another reason behind our approach to the NAE, a more disturbing reason? Is the approach made for purposes internal to the Reformed Church, political purposes (and "political" is not intended as a term of abuse)? That card can be played in a couple ways. Some may desire to unite with the NAE because that is "who we are," or more intentionally, who we "should be." Our presence in the NAE is a lever to move the RCA to a more intentional evangelical posture. Admittedly, some would argue that the so-called "ecumenicals" in the RCA have been trying to move the Reformed Church in other directions, and undoubtedly in the minds of some that may be so. That, however, has not been the stated intention of Reformed ecumenicity, nor, one might add, one that finds expression in actual ecumenical engagement. Another way of playing this card is to maintain that membership in the NAE would pacify a certain wing of the church. This way, the church can

22 *Minutes of the General Synod, RCA,* 1996, 184.

have its cake and eat it too. You might find, in this way of putting the matter, the cynicism of someone who has been through just too many church battles, and you might claim a more benign goal. The Reformed Church will be, as you may rather say, the "bridge" between the ecumenicals and the evangelicals, as the citation from the *Ecumenical Mandate* suggests. The Reformed Church is joining an expanded table. Well, I reply, that is fine, except that it is not a neutral table. In this case the Reformed Church comes to others' table, it accepts their menu, and agrees to act according to their manners. I have no problem with the fact that the NAE has a table and sets the rules. But the Reformed Church is not at an expanded table.

So, the church's approach to the NAE flushes out the "why" question in a new way. But at heart the question is also an old, one may say very old, question, which lurks in the history of a Reformation church. From the outset, the Reformed Church did not claim to be one church among many. It claimed to be the church. It was not, of course, the only church; churches in other places were understood as part of the true church. On the other hand, the church did not originate within the context of a plurality of what we have come to call "denominations." That is an old story and one that does not need rehearsal here.

The "why" question emerged when the old Reformation churches found themselves thrown together in new places where a plurality now exists. Then the question becomes insistent. It is now not, Why should we unite? Instead it asks, Why are we separated? If our unity is from the Father in the Son and through the Spirit, why and how can we live and worship and act separately? For a while we could answer the question historically and pragmatically: immigrant congregations found cultural identity in the churches of their respective heritages. Herman Harmelink has demonstrated how the presence of Dutch Reformed immigrants in the late nineteenth century halted plans for union between the Dutch and the German Reformed.[23]

In fact, this question is embedded in Article 27 of the Belgic Confession, where it is confessed that "we believe and profess one unique catholic or universal Church, which is a holy gathering of true believers in Christ, expecting all their blessedness in him, being washed by his blood, sanctified and sealed by the Holy Spirit." The ambiguity in this sentence moves between the oneness and catholicity of the church on the one hand and the church as congregation on the other. Understanding the church to exist as essentially *congregation* allowed many Reformed to claim themselves as church apart from other gatherings that also claimed to be church. In the Netherlands this would issue in the *Afscheiding*, the separation, a situation that was to replicate itself in the United States.

But the question will not go away. Is it sufficient to talk about "common mission"? Can one do so with ecclesiological responsibility? The unity of the church is not simply a union among believers in some nonembodied manner. The church is the product of the Spirit. And the church is not an invisible reality (if we can even talk in the old visible-invisible dichotomy). The church is (also) institution. To talk of noninstitutional union, at least as a goal, is to commit both pneumatological and ecclesiological docetism. That is, it is to see the work of the Spirit as apart from bodily and institutional expression. And it is to understand the church as a disembodied reality in essence.

To put the "why" in this context is not to challenge the NAE. The church does not appear as something essential in the NAE's statement of faith, but it does in the Reformed. Ecclesiological commitments are part and parcel of what makes the Reformed to be Reformed. Within that context, we are compelled to push the "why" question anew, and that not for the sake of this church's

---

23 Herman Harmelink III, *Ecumenism and the Reformed Church* (Grand Rapids: Eerdmans, 1968), 38-52.

relation with evangelical churches. As a matter of confession, it would be impossible to talk of the *church* engaged in ecumenical relations with individual persons at all! Instead, we ask the question for the sake of the Reformed Church's own identity.

So I conclude. At stake is not how the Reformed Church will get along with evangelicals. It is not even whether the Reformed Church can help create or participate at an "expanded table." At stake is the question of what it means to be church, and whether that question is, as we have confessed, central, not only for the sake of the life and survival of a particular communion, but for the sake of God's reign. If I have been at all successful in these pages, I have provoked you to consider that there is more afoot here than simply reaching out in a new direction, playing nicely in a new ecumenical environment.

10

On Being Evangelical and Reformed:
A Personal Perspective

David Melvin

In the previous chapter, Allan Janssen has discussed some of the important questions at stake in the claim to be both "evangelical" and "Reformed." Here I want to reflect on that claim in more personal terms, speaking from my own heart and life as someone avowedly both evangelical and Reformed.

I begin with a story. In 1999, when I was a member of the staff of the National Association of Evangelicals (NAE), I participated in an international conference in England sponsored by the De Burght Foundation concerning the Russian laws against unregistered churches and ministers—laws enacted to curb mission work in Russia on the part of evangelicals and others. The conference was conducted in English, and the Russian delegates, in explaining and defending their country's laws, depended on the services of a young American translator whom they grew to know and like. He was a military pilot on active duty in Kosovo, who had traded off some of his flight missions there so as to be able to come and help out. As I got to know that young man over the two days of the conference, I discovered that he himself had earlier been a Salvation Army missionary in Leningrad until the authorities there had forced him and his colleagues to leave that city. On the last day of the conference, I had the chance to tell the young man's story to the Russians, and, since they had come to appreciate him as a person and his own quiet witness to his faith, they suddenly saw another side to the issues at hand. There was new understanding because of the testimony of his life, and, to a lesser extent, the testimony of my words.

What does it mean to be "evangelical"? I have begun with this story because I want to make it clear from the outset that although consensus may be elusive, the gospel of the Word—revealed, incarnate and proclaimed—proves faithful and powerful, time and again. As for my Salvation Army missionary friend, and as for the Samaritan woman of John 4, such testimony speaks for itself. First things come first.

Nonetheless, definitions also have their uses, especially in the case of a word like "evangelical," which attempts to name, and so helps us think about, a whole vital way of being Christian.

It is possible to approach the matter sociologically. That is what Mark Noll, Cornelius Plantinga, Jr., and David Wells have done in a collaborative essay that appeared in print a few years ago. They suggest that an "evangelical" will generally be a person who belongs, if Protestant, to a church with origins in the Reformation or in the eighteenth-century awakenings, or, if Catholic, to the neo-Pentecostal wing of the Roman church. But that is not all; to be rightly called "evangelical," persons will also do one or more of the following things: they will "harbor antipathy to modernist naturalism, Kantian idealism and secular humanism," and/or they will display the "optimistic, populist, individualist" marks of American popular culture, and/or they will actively support ministries, societies, etc., whose aim is to spread the gospel.[1]

As far as it goes, that careful characterization of "evangelical" rings true. But in my view it does not go far enough. Evangelicalism

---

[1]   Mark Noll, Cornelius Plantinga, Jr., and David Wells, "Evangelical Theology Today," *Theology Today* 52 (1994-95):496.

is, after all, a genuine expression of Christian *faith*, rather than simply a set of behaviors or attitudes, however characteristic those behaviors and attitudes may be. Consequently, a more explicitly theological approach is called for.

A recent article by Roger Olson entitled, "The Future of Evangelical Theology," comes closer to the approach I have in mind. Olson suggests that true evangelicalism displays four "minimum characteristics," which together serve to define a particular stance of faith: (1) the affirmation of the Bible as "supreme norm of truth"; (2) a worldview in which God—understood as both "transcendent" and "personal"—holds the key place; (3) an emphasis upon the importance of the experience of "the forgiving and transforming grace of God through Jesus Christ"; (4) the conviction that theology's "primary task" is to aid the church in its mission, which is the communication of that message of grace to the world.[2]

Those four points frame evangelicalism as it should be framed, in terms of the essentials of faith. But I would go still one step further, for it seems to me crucial to add that holding fast to the essentials of the faith, as evangelicals do, means embracing precisely the basics of the true faith that the church has always confessed. As Alister McGrath has written,

> Evangelicalism is historic Christianity. Its beliefs correspond to the central doctrines of the Christian churches down the ages, including the two most important doctrines of the patristic period: the doctrine of the "two natures," human and divine, of Jesus Christ, and the doctrine of the Trinity. In its vigorous defense of the biblical foundations, theological legitimacy and spiritual relevance of these doctrines, evangelicalism has shown itself to have every right to claim

---

[2] Roger Olson, "The Future of Evangelical Theology," *Christianity Today,* 9 February, 1998, 40.

to be a modern standard-bearer of historic, orthodox Christianity.[3]

To affirm the authority of the Bible, the love and omnipotence of God, the importance of conversion, and the mandate to evangelize (to follow Olson's list) is perforce to join ourselves to a long tradition that predates the coining of the term "evangelical" in its particular modern sense. The Christian faith, as evangelicals understand it, certainly implies an experience that is deeply felt, of a commitment that is lived out in this present moment—a commitment that adds great power to testimony, as in the case of my friend the pilot. But it also implies an adherence to firm beliefs that can and have been stated objectively throughout a long, continuous history of belief, an affirmation of the abiding truths of the Christian faith. To be evangelical implies therefore to be *confessional*—to confess the ancient Christian faith along with the truly faithful of all times and places, indeed, gladly to confess the object of our faith, Jesus Christ, our Savior and Lord.

Having considered what being evangelical means, I am ready now to consider how it relates to being Reformed. Here I want to tell my own story.

I was raised in a Christian home with eight brothers and sisters by parents with fundamentalist roots. My maternal grandparents attended Moody Bible Institute. My parents attended Wheaton College, where they were classmates of Billy Graham. At the time I was born, my family were members of the Village Church in Western Springs, Illinois, which had been Graham's first call out of college before he became a revivalist. As a young boy, I accepted Christ as my Savior and subsequently was baptized by submersion. Towards the end of my grade-school years, we transferred our church membership to the newly planted Christ's Church of Oakbrook, under the ministry of the Reverend Dr. Arthur H.

---

3   Alister McGrath, *Evangelicalism and the Future of Christianity* (Downers Grove: InterVarsity Press, 1995), 94.

DeKruyter, who had come out of the Christian Reformed Church and is now a colleague in the Reformed Church in America. There, I sensed God's call. During my high school years, I was active in many aspects of church ministry as well as Young Life. Then I was off to Wheaton College, where I graduated with specialties in biblical studies and psychology.

Mine was certainly an evangelical background, and when, after two years in the working world, I enrolled at Gordon-Conwell Theological Seminary in Massachusetts to prepare for the ministry, I certainly thought of myself as evangelical. As for being Reformed, though, at that moment the word was not even in my vocabulary. I remember that, early in my time at seminary, when asked if I was Reformed, I responded, "Heavens no. What's Reformed?"

I was to find out, momentously. At seminary I encountered the Reformed tradition and its way of formulating the truths of the Christian faith. I read Calvin and the great Reformed confessions of the sixteenth and seventeenth centuries. I observed, in various persons at the seminary, great examples of the Reformed commitment to being truly Christian in *all* aspects of life, public and private, individual and corporate. I thoroughly explored the implications of that commitment in evening conversations with my landlord and professor, Dr. David Gordon. As a result of all of this, I discovered that, at my core, I am Reformed. Notice that I do not say that I *became* Reformed. Rather, what I discovered was that in an important sense the Reformed tradition was already my tradition. I had long since received a marvelous Christian heritage from the Village Church in Western Springs and particularly from the solid preaching and teaching that I had experienced at Christ's Church of Oakbrook. I realized that I had known from my youth the life-changing and life-encompassing basics of the Christian faith as, in fact, the Reformed tradition had understood them. I discovered who I was already.

What about my sense of being evangelical then? When I moved with my new wife to Oostburg, Wisconsin, to intern at my first

Orthodox Presbyterian Church, I was very uncomfortable with the term "evangelical." By then the term connoted, for me, an unhealthy over-emphasis on individualistic personal experience, a faith that did not adequately confess the great objective truths of the Christian faith. While I was still at Oostburg and the possibility arose of leaving to join the staff of the National Association of Evangelicals, I resisted at first; since I did not want to be an evangelical, I certainly did not want to be a part of the National Association of Evangelicals. But I sensed God calling me, and I spent a lot of time in prayer and in study of the NAE statement of faith. I came to the realization that if the NAE meant what it said in that statement of faith, it could hardly be accused of weakness in its confession; moreover, that confession was consistent with Reformed doctrine, especially in its affirmation of the authority of Scripture. I also realized that, like it or not, I was still profoundly evangelical—a truth that impressed itself on me at the very first meeting I attended as an NAE staff member. There, joining in prayer with a group of laymen of variety of denominations, I sensed with certainty that these were people of God. The lesson of all of this could not have been clearer: for me, there is no contradiction between being evangelical and being Reformed. I rejoice to be both.

Being both evangelical and Reformed was not a problem for me in the NAE. The association's slogan for years had been "Cooperation without Compromise": we can work together, but we are not going to compromise what we believe. While I was on the staff, Dr. Don Argue, who was then president, led the association of fifty denominations through a change of that slogan. He took the famous motto of Richard Baxter, "in essentials unity, in nonessentials liberty, in all things charity," and changed one word: "in essentials unity, in *distinctives* liberty, in all things charity." I think he caught the essence, in a positive way, of what the old slogan had said perhaps more negatively. Now the message was not, "You and I are going to cooperate in love but please stay away from me on the matters we disagree about," but rather, "You and I are going to cooperate in love and at the same time respect the importance that we each attach to things we may not agree about." In such an atmosphere, I was not just allowed but was positively invited to be both evangelical and Reformed.

I believe I can say the same of the Reformed Church in America. I find in it both the unmistakable, conversion-oriented spirit of evangelicalism, and also the unmistakable, confessional spirit of the Reformed tradition. But even here, we do not agree on everything, and it is the same spirit of charity I found in the NAE that enables us to get along together. If not, for instance, for the "conscience clause" added to the *Book of Church Order* at the time that the ordination of women was approved, I would not now be able to be a minister in the RCA, since my reading of Scripture and my commitment to the authority of Scripture does not allow me to see, at this time, that women should be ordained. On the other hand, being a minister in the Reformed Church of America, I can humbly and gladly submit to the structure, which says that my classis president is a woman, and I can submit to her as head of the classis. Cooperation and unity always require the same spirit of charity.

Now that there is a prospect that the Reformed Church will itself become a member of the NAE, I trust that we will engage the membership of the NAE as Reformed brothers and sisters with the same sensitivity that has marked Reformed Church leadership for years. Feeling so strongly the deep compatibility between the spirit of being "Reformed" and the spirit of being "evangelical," I pray for that "charity in all things" that will allow our whole church to embrace them both.

11

Reformed Protestants and Eastern Orthodox in Dialogue

Karel Blei

Since 1988, the World Alliance of Reformed Churches and the Orthodox Church have been engaged in an official bilateral dialogue. Beginning in 1988, representatives of both world bodies have met every two years for theological consultations. These dialogue meetings have never been prominent events. They have always occurred in the background, far from publicity. It is worthwhile to bring this dialogue to the fore. Why did it start? What were and are the specific problems and difficulties to be overcome? What have been its results so far? These are the questions I would like to address in this essay.

Background: Greek and Latin Traditions

From the point of view of Reformed Protestantism, Orthodoxy is not an obvious dialogue partner. Orthodoxy is eastern Christianity. It had its origin in the Byzantine Empire, the eastern half of the Roman Empire that, up until the fourth century, had enclosed all the countries around the Mediterranean, in eastern and western Europe as well as in northern Africa. In the fourth century, this Roman Empire was divided into two separate parts. The eastern or Byzantine Empire was centered around its capital, Constantinople

137

(today Istanbul). From Constantinople it spread throughout eastern Europe–to Greece, Serbia, Romania, Bulgaria, Albania, Ukraine, Belorus, Russia. In its traditions of thought, the Christianity that developed in this part of Europe was and is typically Greek. Reformed Protestantism originated in the sixteenth century, as part of the broader Reformation movement, in the context of western Christianity, which had developed in the western Roman Empire around its ancient capital, Rome. From there it had spread throughout the central and western European countries. In its traditions of thought, this western type of Christianity has been typically Latin. It has differed from eastern Christianity in more than one way.

The "great schism" of 1054 between eastern and western Christianity, which has never been repaired, was the dramatic outcome of a long development. It was the confirmation of an estrangement that had become increasingly obvious over the preceding centuries. That estrangement also had its impact on the relationship between Orthodoxy and (western) Reformed Protestantism.

Let us consider the background of the schism.

The spirit of Greek culture, predominant in the East, had been characterized by a bias towards philosophical, speculative thinking. The spirit of Latin culture, predominant in the West, had emphasized juridical thinking, clear organization, and the appreciation of logical distinctions. These differences were reflected in Christian theology.

In the East, salvation was seen as a new existence, brought about by the birth of Christ (the "Word of God" "become flesh," the Incarnation) and by his resurrection from the dead. In Christ, it was said, a new way of being human, in immortality, has been offered, in the context of a total re-creation, a cosmic elevation of humankind, which as a result is able to "see" God, to be in touch with God, to be on God's level. As Athanasius of Alexandria put it, "God became Man, in order that Man may become God."[1]

---

[1]   Athanasius of Alexandria, De incarnatione, ed. F.L. Cross (London: S.P.C.K., 1939), par. 54.

The liturgy played a vital role in this understanding. To Orthodox Christians, worship is like heaven on earth. The worshiping congregation is surrounded by icons of Jesus Christ, Mary his mother, the apostles, the saints. These icons are seen as expressions of heavenly reality, an extension of the Incarnation. Worship is therefore experienced as mystical participation in the saving, renewing, elevating event of Christ's incarnation and resurrection.[2]

In the West, theology and the experience of belief have always been much more down-to-earth—less mystical and more juridical in nature. Juridical thinking deals with relations between partners, with issues of contract and covenant, with questions of how to keep relationships in order and how to restore broken relationships, with matters of guilt and of the payment of debts. Here, salvation has been understood as a restored relationship between God and humankind. In this context, the issues of reconciliation and of remission of sins have been of key importance. Attention has focused not so much upon Christ's incarnation and resurrection as upon Christ's reconciling death on the cross, whereby he took away all human guilt. In the context of discussion about these matters, attention has also focused on the nature of human responsibility to God and on the question of what merit can be ascribed to human acts and behavior. Out of these questions the western church developed a system of penance whereby, it was believed, human beings could and should contribute to their own absolution from guilt.

Of themselves, these differences between East and West would not have made a schism inevitable. But they became acute in some very concrete controversies, especially over two issues: (1) the proper understanding of the Holy Spirit, and (2) the position and power of the pope. A few words about each of these issues is in order.

---

2 For a general account of Orthodoxy see Timothy Ware, *The Orthodox Church*, 2nd ed. (Baltimore: Penguin, 1993).

In the Nicene-Constantinopolitan Creed, as adopted by the Ecumenical Council of Constantinople in 381, the Holy Spirit was recognized as, next to God the Father and Jesus Christ the Son, the third revelation of God–or, to use more precise theological terminology, as the third Person of the divine Trinity. As such, the Spirit is God, i.e., "Lord" and "Life-giver." Discussions continued, however, about how to understand the relation of the Spirit to the Father as well as to the Son.

The creed declared that the Spirit "proceeds from the Father." This means that God the Father is the origin of the Spirit; in other words, the Spirit exists only in, and because of, being sent by the Father. But how about the relation of the Spirit to Christ, the Son? Western theologians promoted the opinion that that relation is equally a relation of origin. They emphasized that the life-giving work of the Spirit should be seen as directly connected to the reconciling and renewing work of Jesus Christ. They wanted to exclude the idea that the Spirit brings a new revelation, independent from the revelation in Christ. They were afraid that the idea of such a new revelation through the Spirit would open the door to all kinds of spiritualism and mysticism, which in turn could easily degenerate into wild, uncontrollable fanaticism. Therefore, they wanted to keep the Spirit and the Son closely together and thus to safeguard the personal character of the relation between God and humankind which, as I have suggested, has been a key issue in western theological thinking.

In the West, therefore, the phrase in the creed concerning the origin of the Spirit was amended to read that the Spirit "proceeds from the Father *and from the Son,*" an amendment that, in Latin, required only the addition of a single word, *filioque.* A church synod in the city of Aachen officially adopted this statement in 809; later the pope in Rome agreed.

In the East this development was viewed with alarm. The church in the East considered the church in the West to have taken into its own hands matters that should have been discussed and decided upon by another Ecumenical Council. Moreover, although eastern theologians did not deny the link between the Spirit and Jesus Christ the Son, they emphasized the particularity of the Spirit vis-à-vis Christ, which in their view was obscured by the addition of "*filioque*"; thus for them that addition was not merely inappropriate, but also substantially incorrect. The East maintained the text of the creed as it had been adopted in 381.[3]

The other principal issue between East and West concerned the papacy and its authority. Indeed this second issue overlaps with the first, for it was the pope who ultimately decided on the inclusion of "*filioque*" in the Nicene-Constantinopolitan Creed. But is the pope really the supreme leader of the church? Is the pope in a position to make decisions on behalf of the entire church? In the West, the papal primacy had become an accepted idea, but this was not the case in the East.

Several circumstances had contributed to this divergence. Already in the second century, the bishops of Rome had claimed supremacy over the entire church. They derived their prestige not just from the fact that the city of Rome had long been the capital and the heart of the Roman Empire, but also and above all from the ancient tradition that the apostles Peter and Paul had worked and preached in Rome and had been martyred there. Accordingly, the church of Rome came to consider itself the guardian *par excellence* of the true understanding of Christian faith as preached by the apostles, and the bishops of Rome claimed to be the direct successors of Peter, the leader of the apostles. Later, in the fourth century, the emperor Constantine founded Constantinople as the new capital of the empire, and the imperial court moved there. In the West, as a consequence, the position of the bishop of Rome became even more prominent, as a focal point both for the continuity of Rome's ancient glory and for the actual exercise of leadership. In the western

---

3 On the *filioque* clause see Lukas Vischer, ed., *Spirit of God, Spirit of Christ: Ecumenical Reflections on the Filioque Controversy*, Faith and Order Paper no. 103 (Geneva: World Council of Churches, 1981).

church, moreover, the bishop of Rome had no competitor who could dispute his leading role. But in the East there were other episcopates that claimed preeminence (as "patriarchates"), specifically those of Jerusalem, Antioch, Alexandria, and Constantinople, whose occupants considered the bishop of Rome (the "patriarch of the West") their colleague, even "first among equals," but not their master. Furthermore, when the mass migrations of tribal groups in the years 400-600 caused the collapse of the empire in the West, the western bishops looked for leadership to the bishop of Rome, whose influence thereby was strengthened all the more. This was a crisis not faced by the church in the East, where the empire could defend itself from the newcomers.

It was out of these controversies that the schism between East and West became inevitable. In 1054, Rome and Constantinople condemned and excommunicated eath other.[4] Henceforth, East and West—Orthodoxy and Roman Catholicism—went fully separate ways.

Common Ground?

One might think that this controversy between Orthodoxy and Roman Catholicism would leave Protestantism, and therefore the Reformed tradition, untouched. But that would be a misunderstanding.

The sixteenth-century Reformation was a conflict within the western church. The Reformers were themselves members of the Roman Catholic Church. They developed their newly discovered understanding of the gospel aiming at renewal (reformation) of the western church. When that renewal did not take place, the outcome of the Reformation movement was the existence of separate churches beside, or over against, the Roman Catholic Church.

---

4   For an account of the schism, see Victoria Clark, *Why Angels Fall. A Journey Through Orthodox Europe from Byzantium to Kosovo* (New York: St.Martin's Press, 2000), 17-20.

Nonetheless, these Protestant churches were themselves forms of western Christianity.

The discussions between Roman Catholicism and Protestantism were bitter. The Reformers rejected the Roman Catholic understanding of grace and of the role of the church. They proclaimed the message of the justification of the impious, in Christ, through faith, apart from any human contribution through "merit" or "good works," as the key content of the gospel. Thus their view of salvation conflicted with the Roman Catholic view, and they rejected the notion that the church's sacrament of penance functioned as a necessary condition for salvation.

Yet at the same time, exactly this contrast shows how much the Protestant and the Roman Catholic views are interrelated. The Protestants share the Roman Catholic emphasis on issues of reconciliation and remission of sins. They share the western preference for juridical thinking, in terms of the relationships between God and humanity and between human beings. The terminology is the same, even though it is interpreted in different ways; the questions are the same, even though they are answered in different ways.

That is why the schism between Orthodoxy and Roman Catholicism has its repercussions on the relationship between Orthodoxy and Protestantism. Reformed Protestantism is part of a world—the western world—that is essentially different from the eastern and Greek world of Orthodoxy. Between these two worlds is a wide gap that is not easily to be bridged.

Nevertheless, despite their strangeness to each other, Orthodoxy and Protestantism have certain things in common that suggest another perspective on their relationship. Obviously enough, both Protestantism and Orthodoxy are critical of Roman Catholicism. Orthodoxy criticizes Roman Catholicism because of its openness to new insights and its lack of faithfulness to the ancient, common tradition. To Orthodox eyes, the claim of the bishop (patriarch) of Rome to make binding decisions in matters of faith and doctrine is itself a grave error. This claim has opened the door to the proclamation of new dogmas—not only about the Holy Spirit (in the case of *filioque*) but also about many other things, including the sacraments and Mariology—in contradiction to what for the Orthodox is the church's essential task, namely the defense and maintenance of the unchanging ancient Christian tradition. Although Protestantism has not shared the Orthodox objections against the *filioque* clause (out of the characteristically western concern to keep the Son and the Spirit closely together and safeguard the personal character of the divine-human relationship), it does share the Orthodox mistrust of new dogmas, of ever-developing church doctrine. It also shares the Orthodox rejection of papal primacy. Like Orthodoxy, Protestantism appeals to the origin and source of Christian faith over against later tradition.

There is, of course, a difference here. Whereas Orthodoxy sees this origin in the undivided tradition as proclaimed, presented, and maintained by the first seven Ecumenical Councils (held between 325 and 787) in continuation (as the Orthodox believe) with the apostolic message of the Holy Scripture, Protestants are accustomed to distinguish tradition *from* Scripture. As far as the tradition is concerned, Protestants are always mindful of the possibility of error, whereas the Scripture is seen as infallible, as the only ultimate authority in matters of faith.

Yet one should not over-emphasize this difference. The appeal to the Holy Scripture did not prevent the Reformers from respecting greatly the tradition of the first centuries. Both Martin Luther and John Calvin acknowledged the authority of the church fathers (*patres*), as well as of the early councils and of the ancient creeds. This acknowledgement was rooted in the conviction that the testimony of the early church is in agreement with the Scripture. One sees Calvin's respect for the Apostles' Creed in the fact that in his principal work, *Institutes of the Christian Religion*, he expounds the substance of faith along the lines of the that creed, which indeed provides the work with its very structure. The Reformers recognized the Trinitarian and Christological dogmas of the ancient church as authoritative, because they considered them to be based on Holy Scripture. This recognition was so strong that for them an exegesis of Scripture that appeared to be contrary to these dogmas could not be a correct exegesis. Thus in the Reformed tradition, the dogma is the criterion of the exegesis.[5]

Another point of agreement concerns the relationship between church and peoples or nations. In rejecting the papal claim of superiority over the entire church and so of a centralized church structure, both Orthodox and Protestants, albeit for different reasons, see and maintain a strong connection between church and people. They see the church not as a hierarchical institution that stands above the peoples in their diversity, but rather as an entity that belongs to those peoples. Wherever it developed, the Orthodox church became the national church, safeguarding the national identity of a particular people. Such developments were consistent with the relationship between church and state as it existed in the Byzantine Empire—a relationship of harmony ("symphonia"), in which the church was part of society. The danger of a direct identification of Christian faith and nationalism, or even ethnicism, is always present.

Protestant churches too are churches of their respective nations, churches not *above* but *of* the people. Protestant church structures are at best national structures; Protestants lack an international official synod as an authoritative body. They have also always used the vernacular languages, as over against the universal Latin of the Roman Catholic Church and have been particularly strong in maintaining—as an implication of the Protestant idea of the "priesthood of all believers"—that everyone should be able to read the Bible in his or her own language. Here again, the danger of an

---

5 Jan Koopmans, *Het oudkerkelijk dogma in de Reformatie, bepaaldelijk bij Calvijn* (Wageningen: H. Veenman en zonen, 1938).

identification of Christian faith and nationalism is always present.[6]
Thus, Orthodox and Protestants have more in common than one
might expect at first sight.

Bilateral Ecumenism

The Reformed/Orthodox dialogue is one of the many dialogues
that have been initiated in the last forty years. Generally speaking,
the phenomenon of such bilateral dialogues can be considered one
of the fruits of the Second Vatican Council (1962-1965). At that
council, the Roman Catholic Church decided to engage actively in
the ecumenical movement. One of its main means of doing so was
to seek to establish contacts with other individual church
communions. Thus several dialogues began. This Roman Catholic
enthusiasm for dialogue, moreover, turned out to be contagious;
the church communions who had become dialogue partners of the
Roman Catholic Church also started dialogues among themselves.
Quite a network of bilateral dialogues has emerged, which constitutes
an ecumenical movement in its own right.[7] The World Alliance of
Reformed Churches (WARC) has been one of the partners in this
network, and so has the Orthodox Church. [8]

In such bilateral dialogues, official representatives of two church
traditions meet, in order to try to create conditions under which

---

6   Karel Blei, "The Church: National and Universal: On the Ecumenical
    Relevance of National Church Structures," in *Of All Times and of All Places:
    Protestants and Catholics on the Church Local and Universal*, ed. Leo J. Koffeman and
    Henk Witte. IIMO research publication no. 56 (Zoetermeer: Meinema, 2001),
    19-48.

7   Harding Meyer and Lukas Vischer (eds.), *Growth in Agreement. Reports and
    Agreed Statements of Ecumenical Conversations on a World Level*. Faith and Order
    Paper no.108 (Geneva: World Council of Churches, 1984).

8   For an overview and evaluation of WARC bilateral international dialogues,
    see H.S. Wilson, ed., *Bilateral Dialogues: The Papers and Findings of the WARC
    Consultation Held from April 21-25, 1992 at Princeton Theological Seminary, New
    Jersey, USA*. Studies from the World Alliance of Reformed Churches no. 24,
    (Geneva: WARC,1993).

mutual encounter, communion, or even unification of churches could become possible. The first important thing is to promote a better mutual understanding. By explaining its own position, a delegation participating in a given dialogue can contribute to overcoming possible misconceptions that have been fostered by the dialogue partner, and vice versa. In some cases, as in the relationship between Orthodox and Roman Catholics, mutual doctrinal condemnations have been a hindrance to community. In such cases, the dialogue can help the partners see these condemnations in a new perspective, as the result of a specific situation that no longer exists. The dialogue can contribute to a common appreciation of issues that so far have been assumed to be church-dividing but may not be so in actuality. It can help discover a new common response to contemporary issues of pressing importance.

In some cases, the dialogue partners represent communities that have already much in common. The dialogue will then soon reach its satisfactory conclusion. But sometimes, as in the Reformed/ Orthodox dialogue, a considerable distance has to be bridged. The dialogue will then require much time and patience. In any event, the dialogue result will have to be submitted to the respective mandating bodies. The dialogue delegation itself is not in a position to make decisions on behalf of these sending churches or communions; at best, it can draft recommendations on which the respective official bodies will have to decide.

In order to start a dialogue, both partners must have at least some idea about the meaning of such an enterprise. There must be a certain appreciation of each other—an idea of a common frame of reference, a common language, a common basic understanding. The fact that a Reformed/Orthodox bilateral dialogue could start and continue shows at least a mutual respect of each other's Christian identity. Protestantism and Orthodoxy represent largely unknown worlds to each other, yet each acknowledges the other as a way of being Christian. Each wants to get to know the other better and to explain its own tradition, hoping for comprehension that could bring *rapprochement*.

On the other hand, the composition of both delegations in the dialogue committee is already a clear indication of how different the partners are. The Orthodox delegation consists of official representatives of each of the Orthodox churches in the several eastern European countries. The delegates are metropolitans, bishops, and priests, assisted by some theologians who are experts in ecumenical matters. The WARC delegates, on the contrary, are all theologians; among them are no church leaders or officials—or at least none who are present in that capacity—because WARC itself is not a church, but only an alliance of churches. Unlike the Orthodox Church, the Reformed churches do not engage directly in dialogue but only indirectly, through WARC.

The Reformed/Orthodox Bilateral Discussions

Reformed/Orthodox contacts have been taking place in various parts of the world since the beginning of the twentieth century, in the context of the broader ecumenical movement, the work of Faith and Order and the World Council of Churches. But formal theological consultations arrived on the agenda only in the 1970s. It was professor Thomas F. Torrance of Scotland who took the initiative from the Reformed side. In 1977, on behalf of WARC, he discussed proposals with the Ecumenical Patriarch of Constantinople and with patriarchs of several Orthodox churches. The proposals were warmly welcomed.[9]

The first meeting, which was informal and exploratory, took place in 1979, followed by two more meetings of the same kind, in

---

9   Thomas F. Torrance, ed., *Theological Dialogue between Orthodox and Reformed Churches*, vols.1 and 2, (Edinburgh: Scottish Academic Press, 1985, 1993). Hereafter cited as "Torrance." These volumes contain the text of all the papers and findings of the three preliminary consultations, held in 1979, 1981, and 1983, as well as of the first two official consultations, held in 1988 and 1990.

1981 and 1983 respectively. It was agreed that the official dialogue would concern itself first with "basic theology"—the "fundamental issues in doctrine" that constitute for both Orthodox and Reformed, respectively, the theological foundation for church life and order. In 1979, Torrance, on behalf of the WARC delegation, submitted two memoranda, in which he suggested that

> it would be most helpful if discussions began with the doctrine of the *Holy Trinity*, and then moved from there into the doctrines of *the Son* and *the Spirit*, and then to the doctrine of the *Eucharist*. That would provide the right context for discussion about *the Church and the Ministry*. The conversations could aim at a clarification of the understanding which East and West, in this case the Orthodox and the Reformed, have of their common foundation in the Alexandrian and Cappadocian theology, to which the Conciliar Statements [*i.e.* mainly the Nicene-Constantinopolitan Creed and the Chalcedonian Christological dogma] are so heavily indebted.[10]

The exploration continued in meetings in 1981 and 1983. In these meetings, discussions were held on the issue, "the Authority of (in) the Church," not in order to reach an agreement on ecclesiology as such but rather to clarify the underlying assumptions upon which an official dialogue could start. It had to be clear from the beginning how both Orthodox and Reformed understand authority and its function in reaching doctrinal consensus in the church, so that discussions would be fruitful.

The above quotation shows how much Torrance himself was convinced of the existence of a deep community of Orthodox and Reformed. Reformed faith, in his view, is no less rooted than Orthodox faith in patristic (particularly Alexandrian and Cappadocian) theology—a view that he saw confirmed in Karl

[10] Torrance, 1:10-11.

Barth's christocentric approach to doctrine. He and his fellow delegates strongly wished to make this point clear to their Orthodox dialogue partners. The dialogue could be fruitful if it would take its point of departure in that common foundation.

The Orthodox readily agreed to Torrance's suggestions. The first official dialogue meeting took place in 1988 and the second in 1990. In both meetings, discussion focused on the doctrine of the Trinity. The second meeting concluded with the formulation of an Agreed Statement, the opening sentence of which clearly expresses a conviction of something shared.

> We confess together the evangelical and ancient Faith of the Catholic Church in '*the uncreated, consubstantial and coeternal Trinity*', promulgated by the Councils of Nicaea (AD 325) and Constantinople (AD 381). [11]

In separate sections, the statement successively deals with "The Self-Revelation of God as Father, Son and Holy Spirit" ("It is through the divine Trinity that we believe in the divine Unity, and through the divine Unity that we believe in the divine Trinity"); "Three Divine Persons"; "Eternal Relations in God"; "The Order of Divine Persons in the Trinity" (the "Priority of the Father...within the Trinity does not detract from the fact that the Father is not properly (*kurioos*) Father apart from the Son"); "Trinity in Unity and Unity in Trinity, the One Monarchy"; "The *perichoresis* or the Mutual Indwelling of Father, Son and Holy Spirit"; "One Being, Three Persons"; and "The Apostolic and Catholic Faith."

It is interesting to see how this statement attempts, perhaps even successfully, to overcome the ancient dispute between East and

---

[11] The text has been published in Torrance, 2:219-226, as well as in Lukas Vischer, ed., *Agreed Statements From The Orthodox-Reformed Dialogue*, Studies from the World Alliance of Reformed Churches no. 38 (Geneva: WARC, 1998), 12-17 (hereafter, "Vischer").

West on the *filioque* clause by taking up the essentials of both positions. In the section on *perichoresis,* the text refers to "the mission of the Holy Spirit from the Father" and to "the gift of the Holy Spirit by the Son."

> The Holy Spirit proceeds from the Father, but because of the unity of the Godhead in which each Person is perfectly and wholly God, he proceeds from the Father through the Son. [12]

In the third dialogue meeting, in 1992, the statement of 1990 concerning the Trinity was reviewed and confirmed. The meeting adopted and issued a short commentary that highlighted "significant features" of the statement in what was called "a common reflection."[13] One of the explanatory comments concerns the use of the classical terms "ousia" (divine being) and "hypostasis" (person). God's "being" is to be understood, it is stated, from the biblical name of God, "I am who I am" (Exod. 3:14), which refers to a person rather than to an abstract essence. The "ecumenical significance" of the agreed statement is also pointed out: the Latin theology of the West has traditionally moved from the oneness of God to the three persons of the Trinity, whereas the Greek theology of the East has moved in the opposite direction, but the statement transcends this traditional difference by stressing at one and the same time the Trinity and the unity of God.

In the same meeting in 1992, the discussions continued.[14] Discussion focused now upon the relation between the doctrines of the Trinity and of the Incarnation. Here, a difference of approach became manifest. The Reformed approach starts from "below," by examining the life of Jesus Christ as it is presented in the gospels,

---

12 Torrance, 2:224; Vischer, 16.
13 Torrance, 2:229-232; Vischer, 18-20.
14 The papers and findings of the Orthodox-Reformed Theological Consultations, held in 1992, 1994, 1996, and 1998, edited by George Dion Dragas, appear in *The Greek Orthodox Theological Review,* 43 (1998):205-619 (hereafter, "Dragas").

as the implementation of a threefold ministry or office—that of prophet, priest, and king. From there, one arrives at the doctrines of Incarnation and Trinity: Jesus *is* who he is (the incarnate Son of the Father) because he *does* what he does, as prophet, priest, and king. The Orthodox approach starts from "above," from the Trinity and the Incarnation, and from there considers the life of Jesus Christ as the manifestation of the Word Incarnate.

Connected to that difference in approach was a difference in views about the relation between Incarnation and salvation. The Reformed see the Incarnation as aiming at the work of atonement, accomplished by Christ on the cross, when he bore the sins of humankind. The Orthodox instead place their focus on the Incarnation itself, considering the recapitulation of human nature, as well as of the whole of creation, to be manifested in the perfect human nature of Jesus Christ. More generally, one might summarize the result of the discussion as follows: the Reformed understand who Jesus Christ is (in his two natures, human and divine) from what he does (in his threefold office, in his work of atonement); the Orthodox understand what Jesus Christ does (recapitulating human nature and the whole of creation) from who he is (in the personal unity of his two natures).[15]

Discussions on Christology continued in the fourth meeting, in 1994. Both sides presented papers on "Creation and Incarnation," on the issue of *communicatio idiomatum* (the exchange of properties between the divine and human natures of Christ), and on the relation between "the Christ of history" and "the Christ of revelation." Again, an agreed statement was produced, which addresses the issues discussed in the papers. Unlike the previous Agreed Statement on the Trinity, the Agreed Statement on Christology identifies differences between the Reformed and the Orthodox approaches (which, however, it does not consider

---

[15] Dragas, 339-342.

incompatible), differences that had already come to the fore in the discussions in 1992:

> The Orthodox approach takes its beginning in the Mystery of Incarnation which includes the whole saving economy as it is proclaimed in the Bible, confessed in the Patristic Tradition and experienced in the Divine Liturgy. The starting point of the Reformed approach to Christology and the mystery of the Trinity is the scriptural witness to the life, death and resurrection of Jesus of Nazareth.

In the section on *Communicatio Idiomatum*, it is carefully pointed out, "strictly speaking," that

> the distinct properties of the one nature are not transferred to the other *nature*.... What can be said is that through the *perichoresis* or interpenetration of the two natures in the unity of Christ's person the human nature is restored, sustained and glorified as the *new and perfect humanity* of the last Adam, recapitulating the history of the first Adam. In the Orthodox tradition this is called *theosis* (commonly rendered as 'deification'), but this does not imply that Christ's humanity ceases to be creaturely or becomes divine in essence. Reformed theology shares this understanding, but avoids the language of *theosis*. It treats the theme more in terms of the *sanctification* of human nature in Christ. In both traditions this renewal of our common humanity in the person of the incarnate Word is affirmed and venerated as the decisive saving action of divine grace and the pledge of the renewal and restoration of all who are united to Christ as members of the Body of which He is the Head.

In the section on "Incarnation and Creation," these two are linked closely together:

> The creation is...a deliberate act of God that he might share that love which he is with that which he is not. Creation is

then rooted in the mutual love of the persons of the Triune God. Thus understood, the incarnation is the key which opens to us the intention, plan, meaning and goal of the creation. In the incarnation of the Son the purpose of creation is fully revealed. [16]

In any event, the document does not overemphasize the differences between the Orthodox and Reformed positions. What it highlights is the basic agreement between the two dialogue partners on these matters of Christology.

Taking Stock of the Dialogue

Both the Agreed Statement on the Trinity and the Agreed Statement on Christology were formulated "in a surprisingly short time," as Lukas Vischer, the Reformed cochairperson for the first four meetings, has commented.[17] In *too* short a time? WARC published the statements in 1998, together with four commentaries written by Reformed theologians. Two of these four theologians had not been participants in the dialogue itself. Interesting is the comment by Antonio de Godoy Sobrinho, from Brazil. He criticizes the way in which, in the statement on Christology, traditional terminology is used—e.g., the terminology of the "two natures" of Christ—a terminology that is inadequate "for the total and full human reality of Jesus and, as an historical consequence, for the cross." "In the New Testament," he writes, "we find no indication that in Jesus, the Son of the living God, two 'natures' should interpenetrate hypostatically." Sobrinho furthermore expresses his surprise "at the fact that both the Orthodox and the Reformed simply are content to repeat the text of Chalcedon without adding any criticism whatsoever that might launch a process of renewal in christological reflection." Chalcedon, he says, has been taken as "the last word," instead of (what should have happened) as "a point

16 Vischer, 21-24; Dragas, 433-438.
17 Vischer, 9.

of departure." The Agreed Statement on Christology proposes "an essentially metaphysical Christology" that in the Third World context does not make any sense at all. "A Christology from Latin America would seek to integrate God crucified or God humbled in the person of Jesus into our particular history," he says. "Our christological cry is not concerned with speculating as to how the two 'natures' of Christ interpenetrate."[18]

This comment "from outside" is significant. Whereas the dialogue participants themselves were aiming at reaching a Reformed/Orthodox theological agreement across dividing lines between church traditions, Sobrinho is above all interested in doing theology and confessing Christian faith *vis-à-vis* the burning issues and misery in today's world. In his view, theological discussions that deal with controversies of the past and do not address "our particular history" are totally irrelevant.

In those first four meetings, the WARC delegation was mainly composed of theologians from Europe and the USA. The voice of the Third World was almost entirely absent. In the later meetings, from 1996 on, that situation changed. Representatives from Latin America, as well as from Africa, from the Middle East, and from Asia, have become new WARC delegates. As a consequence, the discussions in these later meetings have become more difficult, but accordingly also more realistic—and because of this, one hopes, they will be more fruitful in the long run.

As one of the WARC delegates in the 1994 meeting—which was my first experience in this context—I remember how it struck me to hear the Orthodox dialogue partners speaking of the church fathers and their theology, and of the Councils of Nicea, Constantinople, and Chalcedon, as if all of this was contemporary, as if many centuries had not passed, as if nothing had happened in the meantime. I learned that this is indeed the conviction of the

18 Antonio de Godoy Sobrinho, "Commentary on the Agreed Statement on Christology," in Vischer, 57-60.

Orthodox. It is exactly what they stand for—the belief that all that matters in Christianity is the tradition of the early church.

Here, the Reformed have a different position. They appreciate and respect the ancient tradition, i.e., the dogmas of the early church. At the same time, they relativize these dogmas in a double way: they see the witness of Holy Scripture as providing the ultimate standard, and they see the the burning issues of today as demanding new responses and therefore requiring continual renewal of theological thinking. That is why such agreements on matters of Trinity and Christology as were produced in the first phase of the Reformed/Orthodox dialogue are less important and less spectacular than one might think. They do not offer a response to the question of what those ancient doctrines might mean today. That question, so important to the Reformed, does not appear to concern the Orthodox at all.

Or are the Reformed too quick in wanting to jump to new conclusions? Should the Reformed be more open to the value and truth of Christian tradition? Is there a way of bringing Christian tradition and modern world together? Could the Reformed learn here from the Orthodox, as the Orthodox can learn from the Reformed? That, I think, is the crucial question for the dialogue as it continues. It is not an easy question to answer, because behind it are precisely the differences between East (i.e., Orthodoxy) and West (including Reformed Protestantism) that I have mentioned earlier regarding how salvation is to be understood. It makes a real difference whether one sees salvation (in the Orthodox way) as elevation, glorification, and *theosis*, or (in the Reformed way) as justification and restored relationship to God and neighbor. But is this difference necessarily church-dividing? Here again, the question is whether Orthodox and Reformed cannot learn from each other.

From 1996 onward, the discussions have dealt with ecclesiology. Papers have been presented, again by both sides, on such issues as the nature of the church, the unity of the church, the church as the body of Christ, the apostolicity of the church, and the role of the sacraments with reference to the church and church membership.

The Reformed participants had hoped that these topics would bring the conversations closer to today's world, but that has been only partly the case. So far, it has been possible to arrive at common statements on ecclesiology only in the form of summaries of discussions and descriptions of the differences between Reformed and Orthodox views. Sometimes it has even been difficult to arrive at such an agreed summary, as when the Orthodox have considered draft descriptions of the Reformed positions to imply misunderstandings of their own position that they have then been eager to correct. The differences of approach to theological issues that had already appeared earlier in the discussions has now become all the more evident: whereas the Reformed approach the church primarily "from below," considering it as the people of God who are called by God, the Orthodox approach it "from above," considering the church as essentially a heavenly, God-given reality.

Again and again, it has not been easy for each side to understand the other. When an agreed statement cannot be reached, the Orthodox tend to criticize the Reformed and feel urged to explain once more the truth of Orthodoxy. The Reformed often have the feeling that their arguments are not really being heard. Deadlocks sometimes ensue.

In September 2002, the eighth official meeting will take place. Again, the theme of ecclesiology is on the agenda. This time, the papers and discussions will focus on the issue of the holiness of the church. As in the discussions on Trinity and Christology, the Nicene-Constantinopolitan Creed is again the point of reference. The "holiness" of the church is, like its "unity," "catholicity," and "apostolicity," among the qualities of the church that are enumerated in that creed. We will see whether our conversations will help us understand each other better and grasp more fully what it means when we confess to believe in "the holy Church."

Will the meeting of September 2002 be the last one? So far, the dialogue has proceeded step by step. There has never been a detailed agenda that would determine in advance when business would be concluded. From the outset, the idea has been to discuss the basics of Christian faith along the lines of the Nicene-Constantinopolitan Creed. Soon the whole list of themes will have been covered.

On the other hand, this dialogue has had a passionate character from its beginning. The dialogue partners do not easily resign themselves to a situation of permanent misunderstandings. Each has the will to come closer to the other, to reach communion. As long as that is the case, as long as there is still hope for progress, and as long as that hope is shared by the respective sponsoring bodies (the Orthodox patriarchates and the WARC executive committee), the dialogue will continue, as a contribution, however modest, to the bridging of the gap between East and West, between Greek and Latin Christianity.

12

New Directions in Faith and Order for the Twenty-first Century: Building a New Common Table

Dale T. Irvin

On April 16, 2001, a letter went out to approximately 325 heads of communions in North America, informing them of a new initiative in Faith and Order.[1] The letter was signed by the three officers of a recently formed Foundation for a Conference on Faith and Order in North America. It briefly explained the initiative that the foundation represents, and the vision and challenge it seeks to address. No individual head of communion or church body was asked in the letter to make a decision for or against the effort to begin to lay a foundation for a faith and order conference in North America, nor was any financial support for the endeavor solicited. The latter stipulation in part precluded the possibility that at a time of budgetary constraints, the foundation might compete with other existing ecumenical bodies for the scarce financial resources offered by the churches. What the letter did ask churches and church leaders to do was to pray for the endeavor as they considered the possibility of a faith and order conference in North America.

---

[1] Copies of this letter and other documents referred to in this essay concerning the proposed Faith and Order Conference can be obtained through the office of William G. Rusch at the Foundation for a Conference on Faith and Order in North America, 99 Park Avenue, Box 298-A, New York, NY 10016.

The letter briefly explained the history that led to its being issued. Eighteen months earlier, a group of individuals committed to the church and its mission had gathered at Princeton, New Jersey, under the sponsorship of the Center for Theological Inquiry (CTI) to reflect upon the future of the ecumenical movement. At the end of that gathering, the consultation in its own name issued a document entitled, "A Call to the Churches for a Second Conference on Faith and Order in North America." Subsequent to that meeting, the organizers of the event circulated the "Call to the Churches" among a number of other church leaders for additional signatures. The "Call to the Churches" was presented to the full Faith and Order Commission of the National Council of Churches of Christ USA (NCCC) at its March 2000 meeting in New York, at which time the commission voted unanimously to endorse it. By early summer the wider circle of endorsements had convinced William Rusch, director of the Faith and Order Commission of the NCCC and one of the key participants in the Princeton consultation, that planning for a conference needed to go forward.

The problem that Rusch encountered as he circulated the call and elicited responses was that no existing institutional body in either the United States or Canada (the two national entities considered within the scope of the initial call) appeared to have what the April 16 letter described as the theological breadth or depth to undertake preparations for such an event. With this in view, Rusch and the leadership of CTI at Princeton convened a second meeting of concerned individuals in January of 2001 to form a nonprofit foundation for the purposes of funding and guiding a faith and order conference in North America. Those participating in that January meeting drew up a constitution with by-laws, adopted an initial budget, formed a board of trustees, elected officers, and appointed William Rusch as executive director. The decision was made that CTI would serve as the financial agent to receive funds until such time as the foundation had its own tax-exempt status.

Why a conference? Why a foundation? Why a new effort in faith and order? These are the questions I think need to be addressed as we talk about constructing a new common table. To do so I will look briefly at several ecumenical trajectories that led us to the present place of faith and order in North America. There are a number of confessional and ecclesiological streams that one can trace from the beginning of the twentieth century: Roman Catholic, Holiness, Pentecostal, Fundamentalist/Evangelical, and Mainline (or "historic," what some call "old-line") Protestant/Eastern Orthodox. Taken together, they constitute a complex ecumenical movement in North America. For reasons that seem largely accidental to me today, that trajectory of old-line Protestant/Orthodox dialogue and cooperation came to be predominantly associated with the term "ecumenical."[2] This is the historical trajectory that is associated with the efforts of the World Council of Churches (WCC), in which the world Faith and Order Commission is lodged. In North America, this stream of history passes through Oberlin, Ohio, where the first North American Conference on Faith and Order was held in September of 1957. The fact that this one stream of institutional history came to be so closely identified with ecumenical work in North America figures into the decision to form the new Foundation for a Faith and Order Conference.

It is important in this connection to note that the story of Oberlin and the first North American Conference on Faith an Order begins with the WCC rather than the NCCC or the Canadian Council of Churches (CCC) in the 1950s. There was no national or continental counterpart to the Faith and Order Commission of the WCC in North America prior to the 1960s. Those familiar with the history of the NCCC will recall that it was formed by the merger of the Federal Council of Churches and a number of other interchurch agencies in the early 1950s.[3] The Federal Council was formed in

2 See Dale T. Irvin, *Hearing Many Voices: Dialogue and Diversity in the Ecumenical Movement* (Lanham, Md.: Univ. Press of America, 1994).

3 The full history of the formation of the National Council and its relation to

1908 as a vehicle for common Protestant social action in the United States. Two years later the World Missionary Conference met in Edinburgh, Scotland. Edinburgh 1910 led directly to the institutional formation of the International Missionary Council (IMC), but indirectly to the institutional formation of a worldwide Faith and Order Movement. One of the U.S. Episcopal Church delegates at Edinburgh was Charles H. Brent, missionary bishop to the Philippines. Stirred by the unity he experienced in the 1910 conference, he took the lead in its aftermath to lay the institutional foundations for the modern Faith and Order Movement.

Faith and Order from the beginning was conceived along ecclesiological lines to be a movement composed of various separated Christian communions from around the world. Churches were asked to commit themselves to the process of Faith and Order without being bound by any of its conclusions. Delegates to the first conferences were endorsed by their churches, although the planners of each event played a significant role in suggesting to a communion who should be appointed. At the same time, delegates never officially represented their communions in the sense of being empowered to speak for them at a formal level. Members of the Faith and Order Movement are free to speak their own minds, although they are expected to do so in a way that is informed by their various traditions and faithful to the beliefs of their various communions. Delegates are expected to report back to their churches on the work of Faith and Order, but no church is bound to accept any decision or recommendation made by such a conference.

The number of communions that joined the Faith and Order Movement is impressive. Even so, a large number of church bodies that were represented at Edinburgh in 1910 and supported the work of the IMC chose not to join the Faith and Order Movement

predecessor agencies, including the Federal Council, is found in Samuel McCrea Cavert, *The American Churches in the Ecumenical Movement 1900-1968* (New York: Friendship Press, 1968), see esp. 204-205.

in those first years. We should also note that until the 1960s there was no Roman Catholic representation in either institution. Rome is still not a member of the World Council of Churches, although since Vatican II the Roman Catholic presence within Faith and Order has grown substantially. The first World Conference for Faith and Order gathered at Lausanne in 1927, the second in Edinburgh in 1937. At both events, the delegates came from member communions in the Anglican, Protestant, and Orthodox traditions. At the Edinburgh conference the decision was made to merge with the closely related Universal Council for Life and Work, which had been organized in the 1920s alongside Faith and Order on a similar methodological basis. The merger of those two institutional bodies took place in Amsterdam in 1948 in the formation of the WCC. Once again, the institution that was formed was conceived as being constituted along the lines of a permanent assembly not unlike the United Nations. The various churches of the world that had sent official delegates to Amsterdam were understood to be founding members of the organization. New communions or denominations could join by applying for membership and being voted into the organization by the representatives appointed by current member churches.

The WCC struggled during its first decade to find an ecclesiological basis for this type of arrangement, whose roots were in the western liberal democratic models of parliaments and leagues of states. The result was a statement entitled, *The Church, the Churches, and the World Council of Churches*, adopted by the WCC Central Committee meeting in Toronto in 1950.[4] The Toronto Statement defined the WCC as essentially a fellowship of churches. No individual member communion was understood or required to change its ecclesiology, or accept another's doctrine of the church as being essentially true. In this regard, the WCC was not to be considered a superchurch or

---

4   The text of the Toronto Statement can be found in W. A. Visser't Hooft, *The Genesis and Formation of the World Council of Churches* (Geneva: WCC, 1982), 112-120.

in any way synonymous with the *Una Sancta* of which the ancient creeds speak. The council was a forum in which various churches of the world could meet one another, study together the issues of unity and mission, and grow toward one another in faith and order more intentionally.[5]

Along these lines the Third World Conference on Faith and Order, by then under the guidance of the Commission on Faith and Order within the WCC, met in Lund in 1952. Lund is noted in ecumenical historiography as marking a decisive shift from the earlier comparative methodology that Faith and Order had employed toward a common search for a deeper Christological and ecclesiological understanding. Two years later, the second General Assembly of the WCC met in Evanston, Illinois. One of the recommendations of Evanston was to encourage the formation of regional study programs to carry further the various ecumenical endeavors springing up around the globe. Responding to this invitation, the U.S. Conference for the WCC took the lead in 1955 in calling for a North American Faith and Order Conference. The task of planning such a conference was turned over to a Committee on Arrangements, which then invited the Canadian Council of Churches and the NCCC to join as sponsoring organizations.[6]

During the summer of 1955, the organizing committee consulted a number of individuals throughout the United States and Canada to arrive at a list of study questions and categories for consideration. Sixteen study groups were then formed on the geographical basis of cities, each group receiving a list of questions to guide its work. Two leaders for each group were appointed by the Committee on Arrangements with the approval of the individuals' various

---

5 For a fuller discussion of the ecclesiological insights and implications of the Toronto Statement, see Irvin, *Hearing Many Voices*, 37-50.

6 Information here and in the following paragraphs is drawn primarily from *The Nature of the Unity We Seek: Official Report of the North American Conference on Faith and Order, Sept. 3-10, 1957, Oberlin, Ohio*, Paul S. Minear, ed. (St. Louis: Bethany Press, 1958).

denominations. No such approval was sought for the rest of the participants in each study group, however. By the summer of 1956, the study groups had completed the first round of their work and were ready to submit their reports to the Committee on Arrangements for consideration. Twelve topics were distilled out of these reports. Each group was then given the task of producing a working paper on one of these topics, and these papers in turn became the starting points for the conference's deliberations.

The second stage of planning entailed selecting delegates to the actual conference itself, a process that began well after the study process was underway. Not until early in 1957 did the Committee on Arrangements (which became the Steering Committee) begin to work with churches to select actual delegates to Oberlin. Many of those selected had not been part of the sixteen study groups working across North America on the preparatory papers, requiring the conference planners to prepare special briefing materials or to assign them to the various existing study groups.[7]

Four hundred delegates, consultants, and observers, drawn from churches in the United States and Canada, eventually gathered at Oberlin in September 1957. All of the churches that at that time were part of the NCCC were represented by delegates that had been appointed or approved by their communions. Four other communions or denominations that were not a part of the NCCC (Polish National Catholic Church, Salvation Army, Evangelical Lutheran Church, American Lutheran Church) sent official representatives as well. Several other churches were represented by individual members who participated in the conference under the category of "observer," without formal recognition by their communion or denomination. In this way, individuals from Southern Baptist churches, the Advent Christian Church, the Lutheran Church-Missouri Synod, the Church of God, the Evangelical Mission Covenant Church, and the Roman Catholic Church

7   *The Nature of the Unity We Seek*, 15-16.

attended.[8] It does not appear that the distinctions among delegates and observers affected the level of participation individuals were allowed to exercise in the conference. The decision was made prior to the conference not to vote on the final reports that each section produced, but simply to receive them and submit them to the churches for their consideration. By this means no individual was forced to vote for or against the positions that the conference took.

On the one hand, gathering such a diverse group of Christians from Protestant and Orthodox communions was remarkable, but the absence of so many others was equally significant. The final message to the churches that the conference issued noted this in a poignant manner. After having applauded the accomplishment of bringing so many together, it continued in a more prophetic vein to state:

> At the same time we are saddened by the absence of members of other churches whom we recognize as fellow Christians, and we ask forgiveness for any failure of charity or understanding in us which may have kept them apart from our fellowship.[9]

I would note the conciliatory tone that the report chose to take. One looks long and hard to find a comparable voice among evangelicals who were engaged at the time in heated polemics directed against the ecumenical efforts Oberlin represented in Faith and Order.[10] The chair of the Oberlin conference, Angus Dun, in a plenary

---

8   In addition to delegates and observers, the Oberlin report includes the
     categories of consultants, stewards, messengers, and staff.
9   "A Message to the Churches," in *The Nature of the Unity We Seek*, 28.
10   See, for example, James DeForest Murch, *Cooperation without Compromise: A
     History of the National Association of Evangelicals* (Grand Rapids: Eerdmans,
     1956); Marcellus Kik, *Ecumenism and the Evangelical* (Philadelphia: Presbyterian
     and Reformed Publishing, 1957); and Bruce L. Shelly, *Evangelicalism in America*
     (Grand Rapids: Eerdmans, 1967), for three significant evangelical voices that
     were addressing ecumenical efforts represented by the WCC and NCCC
     during this period.

address, noted that some who had excluded themselves had done so out of concern that by participating in such an event their witness to Christian truth might be contradicted or obscured. I find that an enormously generous statement of ecumenical charity and concern. One can almost hear a note of anguish in his words.

But however generous the tone, the fact remains that more churches and more Christians were not represented at Oberlin than were. The *Yearbook of American Churches* for 1957 lists more than two hundred Christian communions or denominations.[11] I find no mention in the report from Oberlin, and have seen no evidence in the various denominational records of these other communions, that any were contacted or invited to consider whether they could play a role in some capacity. The two Roman Catholics observers who attended (Fr. Gustave Weigel, SJ., of Woodstock College and Fr. John B. Sheerin, a Paulist priest who edited *Catholic World*) were appointed by the archbishop of Cleveland as his representatives.[12] There were no Pentecostals at Oberlin, and only a few people with any connections to churches associated with the conservative evangelical wing of American Christianity. The absence of these voices diminished the overall value of Oberlin's achievements.

Following Oberlin, the decision was made to locate a Department of Faith and Order Studies within the NCCC in the USA. In 1964 a new Division of Christian Unity was formed, with the Department of Faith and Order lodged within it. By 1970 the department was ready to be redefined officially as a commission, organized along lines of the Faith and Order Commission within the WCC. That is pretty much how things continue today. There is a Faith and Order Commission within the NCCC that is made up of individuals officially representing various churches or communions, several of which are not members of the NCCC itself. Individuals who come from communions that are part of the NCCC are approved by the General Assembly of the NCCC as well as by their various

---

11 The *Yearbook* continues to be published by the NCCC.
12 Cavert, *American Churches in the Ecumenical Movement*, 233.

churches, while those who are from churches that are not members of the NCCC are selected by the Faith and Order Commission itself.

What about these other churches that remain outside the formal structures of the NCCC? Have they been without ecumenical consciousness, or deaf to our Lord's prayer for unity? If one believes, as I do, that the ecumenical impulse is fundamentally an expression of the Spirit's working among us, then to say that particular churches have been without an ecumenical consciousness would be to say that the Holy Spirit has not been at work among them. I would suggest instead that the ecumenical impulse comes to expression in different ways among various congregations and communions, shaped by the historical conflicts and tensions that we have witnessed being lived out across the last century, and informed by different understandings and commitments regarding the gospel. We can certainly debate the adequacy of these various expressions. But if there is any lesson to be learned from the last one hundred years of ecumenical history, it is that ecumenism cannot be reduced to the efforts of institutions such as the WCC, the NCCC, or the Faith and Order Commission. Indeed, it is now commonly said that institutions such as the WCC or NCCC do not represent the extent of the modern ecumenical movement. Many within the WCC like to say it that it is still the privileged instrument of the ecumenical movement, or a privileged instrument of ecumenism. But everyone seems to be recognizing that there is more to the ecumenical movement than what has transpired within those instruments or agencies that identify themselves as the major vehicles for modern ecumenism.[13]

This is what brings us to the discussion about "building a new common table." In ecclesiological terms, the table is the place around which we gather as the household (*oikos*) of God.[14] The

---

13 See Irvin, *Hearing Many Voices.*
14 A number of years ago I was involved in a regional study of the legal definition of the "familly" that is written into zoning laws in communities around

unifying center of the life of fellowship, it is the place where most of us meet the Risen Christ in worship.[15] It is also a metaphor that reminds us of the place where we need to serve the poor. In social life the table is often the place around which negotiations happen, and thus it can represent a place of political or institutional encounters as well.

In recent years, at both the international and national institutional levels of so-called "ecumenical life," we have been hearing about the desire of some to extend the ecumenical table to make room for others who are not currently sitting at it.[16] I am uneasy with such statements not because I am opposed to a more inclusive ecumenism but because of the assumption about where the ecumenical table is actually located. The problem is, simply put, that there is not one ecumenical table and there never has been. The very nature of ecumenism ought to have alerted us to the fact that there are multiple ecclesial and ecclesiastical tables at which Christians sit. There are different rules for sitting, and different understandings of what it even means to be sitting at them.

The question then is not so much about how large we can make a particular table, but about learning how to sit at tables that others have been at work constructing and setting, under the prompting of the Holy Spirit, for more than a century. This suggestion cuts both ways—even multiple ways—simultaneously. Evangelicals,

Philadelphia. In many older towns, the legal definition of family was not "one or more persons related by blood or marriage," the more common recent definition, but "any group of persons who share a common table," a definition that was suited to the earlier rural practice of households including boarders and workers. I think this older definition of family is one that conforms to the Christian understanding of the *oikos* of God.

15 I am acutely aware of the theological tensions invoked by referring to the center of eucharistic life as a table rather than an altar. There is no reason why one word need displace the other in our sacramental theology, however, as each offers important insights into the manner of grace we experience in the eucharist or Lord's Supper.

16 See Dale T. Irvin, "The Banquet of Ecumenical Theology," *Ecumenical Review* 43:1 (1991), 68-78.

Roman Catholics, Pentecostals, and others need to learn to sit at the so-called mainline ecumenical table set by the NCCC and its member communions; but those who are comfortable sitting at that table need desperately to learn how to sit at a table spread by evangelicals or Pentecostals, while Pentecostals and "mainline" ecumenicals need to learn to sit at a Roman Catholic table, and so on.

What I am suggesting is a model of ecumenism that does not perceive, for the immediate future at least, the construction of a single, common table. I think we need instead to spend a significant period of time learning to sit at several different tables. No single one of us will be able to become accomplished at sitting at the entire range of ecumenical tables that are now being set. What we need is a cadre of fraternal and sororal workers, of cross-communion missionaries working together to transform or renew the churches.

This is where the Foundation for a Faith and Order Conference comes in. First, those who have been working toward it have set in motion a project designed to generate the minimum of bureaucracy. No new ecumenical structure or organization is planned or envisioned. The foundation is not a new NCCC or National Association of Evangelicals. It is not a new council. It is a vehicle for setting in motion the study project in a manner designed to cross the multiple ideological, theological, and ecclesiological boundaries that now exist. I honestly expect that if the foundation does its job well, it will no longer be needed after the conference itself takes place in 2004. (I should note that I have heard of no one on its board saying that as directly as I do; it is simply the inference I am drawing from the manner in which the foundation has been formed.) Its support will have to come from churches, schools, organizations, foundations, and individual donors, and in the form of funding as well as in-kind services.

The board of the foundation itself is made up of the presidents of three very different seminaries, several bishops (one who is a cardinal archbishop, one who is a metropolitan), members of the

Faith and Order Commission of the NCCC, officers from ecumenical agencies, several other prominent theological educators, and at least one person who pastors a local congregation. They are Roman Catholic, Eastern Orthodox, Anglican, old-line Protestant, evangelical Protestant, and Pentecostal. They do not pretend to represent adequately the entire range of ecumenical voices active in North America today. The kind of representational ecumenism that has been advanced along the lines of liberal democracy is by its very nature restrictive, for it depends upon some presupposed definitions about who and what deserves to be represented and thus conceals the decision-making powers that operate behind the scenes. They do intend to create the context for new kinds of conversations that will challenge us all to rethink what ecumenism might mean for the next generation of church leaders in North America.

Second, those who have been involved in laying the foundation for a second Faith and Order Conference in North America recognize that the planning needs to engage existing streams of ecumenical life in churches, schools, theological centers, scholarly societies, and study groups in a variety of new ways. For this reason the initial consultation designed to inaugurate the study process that will lead toward the conference itself was planned with an open-ended agenda.[17] The consultation, which took place at Notre Dame in October 2001, sought to facilitate an open conversation

17 The initial planning consultation was held at the University of Notre Dame Oct. 7-9, 2001. Approximately 125 persons from the United States and Canada attended, representing mainline Protestant, evangelical Protestant, Roman Catholic, Pentecostal, Holiness, and Orthodox church traditions. The Notre Dame consultation, arguably one of the most ecumenically diverse consultations on faith and order ever held in North America, affirmed the decision to call a conference and began the process of building the new ecumenical connections necessary for such an event to take place. Copies of the "Final Report from Notre Dame" and other information on the process to date are available from the foundation office listed above, or from the foundation press officer, Jean Caffey Lyles, by email at FOconf2005@aol.com.

regarding the tensions that are involved in ecumenical conversations today, engaging individuals from a broad range of ecclesiastical locations and ecumenical commitments. What are the issues that need to be studied regarding matters of faith and order in North America today? What must such a conference address regarding the unity, identity, and mission of the church in the future? Where are such matters already being addressed, and by whom? How can those who are currently engaging in relevant work be encouraged to work with others to bring their insights to a second conference in North America?

One of the more helpful concepts or images for me for understanding the ecumenical movement over the past century is that of the transit lounge.[18] Ecumenical work takes place as a conversation in a transit lounge, a space where people who are traveling on different journeys are intentionally offered an opportunity to meet and engage one another in a significant way. Lest I be accused of being an elitist for offering an image that presupposes that one engages regularly in airline travel, let me offer another that has guided my thinking: the image of a crossroads. Ecumenics is nothing more than how we deal with the strangers whom we encounter at the crossroads of our journeys.[19] The first step toward showing hospitality to the stranger is to recognize him or her as such. This means neither reducing the stranger to one's own existing paradigms nor ignoring the stranger and treating him or her as invisible. Concomitant to that is recognizing one's own self to be a stranger in the other's presence and behaving accordingly

---

[18] I have borrowed the image of ecumenical theology as a conversation taking place in an airport transit lounge from Werner Simpfendörfer's reflections upon a 1984 WCC symposium at Cartigney, Switzerland, found in Thomas Weiser, ed., *Whither Ecumenism? A Dialogue in the Transit Lounge of the Ecumenical Movement* (Geneva: WCC, 1986), x.

[19] Dale T. Irvin, "Towards a Hermeneutics of Difference at the Crossroads of Ecumenics," *Ecumenical Review* 47:4 (Oct. 1995), 490-502.

as a guest at another's table, not as if one owned the only table worth sitting at.[20]

I think we need a period of visitation and mutual learning for new collaboration before we talk about what the new ecumenical table will look like in North America. Whatever new ecumenical table we eventually construct is going to exclude someone. That is virtually inevitable, given the historical limitations of the church and the sinful nature of the world that we live in. Some of us are convinced that we currently sit at that table when we gather for the eucharist. Others of us grasp the table by faith as being a spiritual or eschatological reality that is not yet to be found in any currently existing church structure. Some are concerned to maintain the purity of the table around which we are called to sit, while others find the table can be set only in the presence of the poor, or in the cause of justice and mercy. A few continue to alert us that the table is being set in surprising places where the Spirit now is moving. What we can be sure about is that we should not become too attached to any particular table as it is being set just yet. I do believe there is one table at which we will all sit some day. I don't doubt that some of these earthly ecclesial tables around which are now gathered resemble that Great Table more than others. I think we are all being renewed only by the hope of sitting at that ultimate place where these questions will finally be resolved.

---

20 For an excellent sociological and theological examination of the meaning of the stranger, see Victoria Lee Erickson, "The Stranger is the Friend: A Reterritorialized Simmel and Washington," *Union Seminary Quarterly Review* 52:1-2 (1998), 109-128.

13

The Waters of Baptism and
the Streams of Ecumenism

Wesley Granberg-Michaelson

When I grew up in an evangelical, nondenominational church, we sang a children's song that some readers may remember: "Deep and wide, deep and wide, there's a fountain flowing deep and wide." Little did I realize that those words provide a vivid picture of the Reformed understanding of the one true church, as well as portraying the present dilemma of the ecumenical movement. Neither "Reformed" nor "ecumenical" was part of my common vocabulary of faith until I entered Hope College. But today, the memory of that chorus, with its hand motions, paints an impressionistic picture of what "Reformed" and "ecumenical" might look like as we enter the twenty-first century.

Today, that fountain is flowing through the waters of baptism more widely than ever before. The diverse geographic, cultural, linguistic, and ethnic expressions of Christ's body in our contemporary world are overwhelming. These waters are breaking through floodgates of historical understanding, ecclesiological classification, and ecumenical structure. If we are open, attentive, and honest about these realities, we are left either perplexed about our ecumenical calling, or in awe at the fecundity of God's Spirit, or perhaps both.

Let us be sure that we are clear about the situation. We need go no further than a recent *Newsweek* article, "The Changing Face of the Church," in which Kenneth Woodward reports:

- •"Christianity is spreading faster" in Africa today "than at any time or place in the last 2,000 years";
- "in 1900—the beginning of 'The Christian Century'— 80% of Christians were either Europeans or North Americans. Today 60% are citizens of Africa, Asia, and Latin America";
- "the Republic of Korea now has nearly four times as many Presbyterians as America";
- America and Europe are regarded as "mission territories" by churches in the "South," who are sending their missionaries and evangelists; and that
- "to millions of Christians in Asia and Africa, the words 'Protestant' and 'Catholic' inspire little or no sense of identification."

But most astonishing is this simple fact: "According to David B. Barrett, co-author of the *World Christian Encyclopedia*, there are now 33,800 different Christian denominations. 'And the fastest-growing are the independents, who have no ties whatsoever to historic Christianity.'"[1]

Allow that number to sink into our Reformed, ecumenical consciousness. Consider this. The World Council of Churches, working for more than fifty years as the primary instrument for Christian unity, today has grown to about 340 member churches. In other words, if Barrett's figures are anywhere near accurate, the

---

1 Kenneth L. Woodward, "The Changing Face of the Church," *Newsweek*, 16 April 2001, 48-49. Cf. David B. Barrett, George T. Kurian, and Todd M. Johnson, *World Christian Encyclopedia* (Oxford and New York: Oxford Univ. Press, 2001), 1:3-19.

WCC comprises about 1 percent of the total number of Christian churches that now occupy the world scene. Indeed, there is a fountain flowing, and it is very wide—wider than we have ever imagined. And these waters of baptism have overflowed the traditional streams of ecumenism. They now are rivers running wild, and God only knows where.

It is no wonder, then, that the points of ecumenical creativity and promise are found today at the periphery of traditional ecumenical agendas and structures, rather than at their center. That means, of course, that the center is shifting: certainly from the North to the South, evidently from conciliar reflection to missional engagement, and probably from the second person of the Trinity to the third.

Let's consider some small signs of such future ecumenical ventures and reflect on the role of a Reformed presence in their midst. Notable, for example, is the dialogue between the World Alliance of Reformed Churches (WARC) and the Organization of African Instituted Churches (OIC). Gregg Mast has given us his illuminating analysis in chapter eight.

An estimated twelve hundred churches are started in Africa every month. Most take root in indigenous soil with charismatic leadership often inspired by particular visions and images or verses of Scripture. One can only imagine the issues of polity, liturgy, theology, biblical interpretation, and understandings of gospel and culture that eventually emerge within these settings. The most important response from more "historic" churches, both within Africa and without, is for avenues of communication and relationship to be sought wherever possible.

Formal ecumenical structures, especially as developed by historic churches on basically Western patterns, are nearly irrelevant at this stage to these newly emerging churches. The ecumenical task is one of nurturing space where relationship can grow. The WARC-OIC dialogue is one small but hopeful example, and the Reformed Church in America is privileged to be the sole non-African participant in this conversation.

In Latin America, the grass-roots realities of the churches are impinging on existing ecumenical institutions. The historic Protestant churches of the region formed the Council of Churches in Latin America, called CLAI, in 1978. Today it is struggling to open its life to the fast-growing Pentecostal churches that have dramatically altered the ecclesiological climate of Latin America in the past two decades.

The general secretary of CLAI, Israel Batista, a friend and former colleague of mine on the staff of the World Council of Churches (WCC), has been determined to build a serious dialogue with Pentecostals, inviting them into this fellowship. Many traditional ecumenists have resisted the process. In a recent e-mail to me, Israel said this:

> Sometimes it is hard to open spaces, mainly among some churches (the minority) who have lost the mystic and want to keep the ecumenical movement tied to old patterns, like a "club of enlightened people." However, the grace of Lord is immense....After two years, CLAI has opened new spaces among churches never before related to the ecumenical movement....In these two years we have tried to bring CLAI closer to the life of the churches, to enable new biblical and theological debates and to open our churches to the needs in our societies. Many beautiful stories have been written. Slowly we are moving into a new momentum for the life of the churches in Latin America. I am completely sure that the Spirit of God is with us in this task.

Carlos Tamez, a professor at the Presbyterian Theological Seminary in Mexico, says that Latin American church leaders "have to read the new faces of the churches in Latin America." Tamez is clear about the challenge that is posed:

Pentecostal faith offers a lot to the historic churches. It can help us discover new dimensions of the gospel. Bit by bit historic churches have been parking themselves in a liturgical, doctrinal, and disciplinary structure that has prevented us from fully living out the Gospel. Pentecostal faith helps us get closer to the spirituality of the people, the poor. We need to embrace it, carefully and with analysis, but nonetheless embrace this other dimension of the Gospel that has been absent in our churches.[2]

A member of the executive committee of CLAI, Verona Haynes, referring to the "confusion and uncertainty" inherent in the process, has said of the opening worship of CLAI's recent assembly, "We didn't know if it was Pentecostal or historic or Neo-pentecostal or what."[3] I am reminded of Gregg Mast's comment to me at the end of the opening worship for the Mission 2000 celebration at the time of the General Synod of 2000. "Well, we made it through," he said. "I'm not sure what it was, but we made it through."

Two decades ago, ecumenists in the West looked to Latin America as the source of liberation theology, declaring an option for the poor. Today ecumenists in Latin America are recognizing that Pentecostal churches have become the option of the poor. Indigenous expressions of Pentecostalism (unlike some western, televised imports) have strength precisely because of the solidarity of local congregations with the daily life and struggle of the people.

It will take time, creativity, and spiritual relinquishment if the many movements on the periphery of traditional ecumenical structures are to transform the core of ecumenical reality and life. Many committed ecumenists from the North and South alike are protective of entrenched ecumenical agendas and habits. But the fountain is overflowing, far wider than ever before.

2 Quoted by Paul Jeffrey, in "Pentecostal Blessing or Threat? A Challenge to Latin American Ecumenism," *Ecumenical News International Bulletin,* 31 January 2001, 28.
3 Quoted in ibid., 27.

Once a year I try to fish in Yellowstone National Park. The Lamar River flows through the northern valley and wide meadow of that protected land. After the severe winter, powerful spring runoffs surge through the valley—so powerful, in fact, that the actual path and streambeds of the river will move and change.

That's what I think ecumenism is like today. The waters of baptism, flowing wide, are changing and altering the streams of ecumenism. The question is whether we will adjust or remain where we are, fishing in streams that have become shallow and dry because the water is now flowing elsewhere.

In that song of my childhood, we also sang that the waters of the fountain are flowing deep. That is the other challenge for us in the Reformed family, specifically in the Reformed Church in America, to consider as we engage in the broad ecumenical arena now and in coming years. How is ecumenical fellowship made deeper?

This task has become clearer in recent years, especially in the life of the World Council of Churches. Its process of "Common Vision and Understanding of the WCC" evolved into fruition through most of the past decade. The process clarified that at its core, the WCC exists as the fellowship of its member churches with one another. It is not a service organization, or a nongovernmental international bureaucracy, or a global church program agency. While its structure may exhibit some of those features, the heart of the council is the fellowship of its member churches, and all that this requires and inspires.

This insight, of course, focused attention on the present quality of such fellowship. For a variety of reasons, the place and role of the Orthodox churches within the WCC's fellowship has become a matter of urgent concern. A special commission has been formed, comprised equally of Orthodox and other member church representatives of the WCC, to address and, it is hoped, resolve this relationship.

The pressing questions of this process are worth noting, for they have an impact upon us as well: (1) How do we fairly express membership in the WCC, especially since Orthodox churches by nature are set in number, and Protestant churches constantly proliferate? (2) How are decisions made in this fellowship, and can models of discernment and consensus be used rather than those of Western parliamentary procedure and majority voting? (3) How can we worship and pray together, especially when some churches do not necessarily recognize other churches as part of the one true church? (4) How can we arrive at shared understanding(s) of what it means, ecclesiologically, for a member church to belong to the fellowship of the WCC? (5) How can controversial social, moral, and political issues be discussed in ways that do not damage or break this fellowship?[4]

One can see how this agenda of issues is not completely distant from the challenges facing the General Synod of the Reformed Church in America.

At the relational bottom line, Orthodox churches wonder how Protestant churches can be part of the fellowship of the WCC but remain so institutionally divided from one another, even within confessional families. Protestant churches, on the other hand, wonder how true fellowship can be sustained as long as Orthodox churches do not recognize us, in some way, as authentic expressions of the church.

Beneath the pressing questions on the agenda of the special commission, in my judgment, lies the understanding of baptism for our participation in ecumenical fellowship. What may seem simple to some is profound for others.

Do we, in fact, accept one another's baptism? In the fellowship of the WCC, this question has never been answered. In the discussions leading to and arising from the *Baptism, Eucharist and Ministry* document of 1982, we have considered what baptism means for each of us as churches, but not what it then means for our fellowship together.

---

4   World Council of Churches Central Committee, *Minutes of the Fifty-first Meeting* (Geneva: W.C.C., 2001), 68.

Past decades—and even past centuries—have witnessed many ecumenical discussions about the meaning of the Eucharist. Protestants have often pressured for Eucharistic sharing in ecumenical contexts, sometimes in ways that suggest little understanding of the ecclesiology of other churches.

But around the baptismal font, we could find ourselves in a different and more promising situation. This fountain does flow deep. Reflecting together on the waters of baptism offers hope for deepening the streams of ecumenical fellowship that we presently share.

In this light, the results thus far of the Presbyterian Church (USA) dialogue with the Pontifical Council on Christian Unity, in which the RCA is privileged to be an invited guest, are all the more significant. The recent encounter in Rome, which included a private audience with Pope John Paul II, affirmed the prospect of a Reformed response to the Lutheran-Roman Catholic *Joint Declaration on Justification*, as Anna Case-Winters has told us in chapter seven. But perhaps even more importantly, that encounter agreed to explore "the possibility, at the appropriate level, of reaching a mutual recognition of the sacrament of baptism."[5] Such a step, if successfully achieved, would transform the official ecumenical relationship between the Roman Catholic Church and the Presbyterian Church (USA). Certainly the Reformed Church in America could be included in that process. This should be one of our priorities in our future ecumenical initiatives.

In some places—again, on the periphery—such breakthroughs around baptism are already in practice. At places in Australia, for instance, common baptismal certificates are printed that state on the reverse side that this baptism is officially recognized by the Orthodox Church, the Roman Catholic Church, the Uniting Church

5 "Joint Statement of the Presbyterian Church (U.S.A.) Delegation and the Pontifical Council for Promoting Christian Unity, March 27, 2001." The statement is currently available through the Presbyterian News Service, at http://www.pcusa.org/pcnews/oldnews/2001/statement.htm.

in Australia, and other denominations. In such cases, the church's one baptism is not just preached as an ideal; it is practiced (and printed) as a visible reality.

In the liturgy of the Reformed Church in America, we say exactly the right thing when we declare that upon baptism a child is "received into the visible membership of the holy catholic church." But what are we doing in local settings to give practical, tangible expression to that powerful truth?

At the World Council of Churches Eighth Assembly in Harare, Zimbabwe, during December 1998, the Program Guidelines Committee, outlining future work for the WCC, directed that all the member churches of the WCC be engaged around four central questions. One of them was this: "How do we understand baptism as a foundation for the life in community to which we are called to share together?"[6]

At the WCC Central Committee meeting in Potsdam, Germany, earlier this year, a similar request was made, urging that the member churches explore what baptism means for our participation in the fellowship of the WCC.[7] Thus far, since the Harare Assembly, nothing has been done to implement such requests. Other priorities, agendas, and habits seem to occupy the limited capacity of the WCC's staff. But we can hope that this might change, and in the meantime we can encourage practices in consistory, classis, regional synod, and General Synod that act out what we believe about one common baptism into the Holy Catholic Church.

The day after Palm Sunday last year, an article in the *Chicago Tribune* told about two congregations—one Episcopal and one Roman Catholic—on the south side of the city:

> The congregations of St. Elizabeth Roman Catholic Church and St. Thomas Episcopal Church met for the eleventh

---

6   Diane Kessler, ed., *Together on the Way: Official Report of the Eighth Assembly of the World Council of Churches* (Geneva: W.C.C. Publications, 1999), 149.
7   *Minutes of the Fifty-first Meeting,* 117-18.

straight year for a combined blessing of the palms. Rev. Martini Shaw of St. Thomas said the saddest part of the ceremony for the two predominantly African-American congregations is when their processions go separate ways for church services. "We can't share the Eucharist," Shaw said, "but we can share those things we have in common. Baptism being one of them, and also recognizing the narrative of Jesus entering Jerusalem on Palm Sunday."[8]

Well, we can add that, ecumenically, one thing leads to another. The important task is to get first things first, as these congregations seem to have done. Then it is not hard at all to imagine the day when those two processions remain together, all the way to the Table.

What, then, do these reflections suggest for us to do as we consider the future presence of the Reformed Church in America at the ecumenical table?

First, practice humility. Amidst the 33,800 denominations flowing today from the waters of baptism, the Reformed Church in America is, after all, a tiny trickle. Since we are "reformed and always reforming," we should expect that God still has much to teach us through relationship and participation with the diverse expressions of Christ's body. My sense is that much of what we will learn will come around the missional engagement of the global church today. Here, the RCA's principle of always carrying out mission activities in partnership with other churches in local settings can become a rich ecumenical resource for our own learning, growth, and reformation.

Second, be in dialogue with the whole church. Within the past two years, Gregg Mast has journeyed to Lagos to talk with African Instituted Churches, Steve Brooks (then General Synod vice president) has gone to Fuller Seminary for a WCC dialogue with world evangelicals, Doug Fromm has talked with the pope in Rome, and I have traveled

8   Mickey Ciokajlo, "Faithful Mark Palm Sunday," *Chicago Tribune*, 9 April 2001, sec. 2, p. 3.

to Damascus for conversations with the Orthodox. We are a small denomination, but our ecumenical reach is broad, as it should be, because of what we say whenever we accompany someone to the baptismal font. This fountain flows deep and wide, and we should go where these waters flow.

Third, model an inclusive, open ecumenical style. Our most recent step to do so is our application to join the National Association of Evangelicals (NAE). This lengthy process led the NAE to change its bylaws, removing language that prohibited membership by churches who belonged to the NCC or WCC.

Something important is being modeled here. Evangelical and ecumenical commitments should never be mutually exclusive. Streams of ecumenism that can receive the waters of baptism flowing in the world today will never be separate channels. Ecumenical initiatives in the twenty-first century will not be zero-sum games—choices between Pentecostals or Catholics, between Evangelicals or Orthodox, or, closer to home, between the Reformed Church in America and the United Church of Christ.

Since our history and character as a denomination, for whatever curious reasons of both sin and grace, enable us to be the first denomination to belong both to the NCC and NAE (assuming the acceptance of our pending application), then we should embrace this providential opportunity with joy. Our ecumenical mandate, approved unanimously by the General Synod in 1996 after years of work, includes this direction:

> We will give particular attention to building ecumenical bridges of fellowship and partnership between conciliar bodies and 'evangelical' churches and agencies, in order to enhance the healing of our divisions for the sake of our common witness.[9]

Implementing this goal is a modest yet notable service toward building a wider ecumenical table in the United States. That task has

---

[9] *Minutes of the General Synod of the RCA*, 1995, 184.

become a courageous priority for the National Council of Churches of Christ. It has declared its willingness to be part of a costly but creative search for a new ecumenical vehicle, inclusive of Catholics, Evangelicals, mainline Protestant churches, historic black churches, and the Orthodox Church. The Reformed Church in America can offer the contribution of its own witness and commitment to the task of envisioning and creating such a table of fellowship.

In closing, I turn again to words from the Program Guidelines Report of the WCC's Harare Assembly, calling for "an ecumenism of the heart":

> The one ecumenical movement is not, first of all, about programs, structures, and cooperation. Rather, the foundation of all our ecumenical engagement is our response to God. It asks for nothing less than the conversion of our hearts. Because ecumenism is directed towards God, and to the world so loved by God, worship and spirituality must take even deeper roots in the heart of all we do....the only sustaining path towards the heart of the unity we seek leads us together in worship, prayer, and shared spiritual life."[10]

Let me share a story. Four years ago, a group of so-called "heads of communion" from NCC member churches began going on periodic retreats with one another, not to discuss the problems of the NCC or other business, but to deepen our fellowship. Each retreat begins with a couple of our number sharing their spiritual autobiographies. Then we enter twenty-four hours of silence, in which we pray for one another and for our churches, and try to listen. Following this, we share in an act of worship together – one time a foot-washing service, another time communion. The dozen or so who have participated would say that more has happened in those retreats to strengthen our ecumenical commitment than all the other various meetings and conferences we attend.

---

10 Kessler, *Together on the Way,* 143.

"Deep and wide, deep and wide, there's a fountain flowing deep and wide." The future ecumenical commitment of the Reformed Church in America, with all our partner churches, will best be nurtured by discovering how we can be spiritually present and open to these deep and wide waters of baptism. They are flowing in rich and diverse ways from this fountain of life, creating new streams that can nourish the life, witness, and service of Christ's one body in a world so loved by God.

Index